T0268256

CRAFT

The Eat Fit Guide

CRAFT

to Zero Proof Cocktails

By Molly Kimball, RD, CSSD with Ethan Skaggs

Edited by Melanie Warner Spencer

Photography by Hope Frugé

PELICAN PUBLISHING

NEW ORLEANS

ISBN 9781455626908
Ebook ISBN 9781455626915

Printed in Korea
Published by Pelican Publishing
New Orleans, LA
www.pelicanpub.com

To Chef Carl Schaubhut, who continues to inspire us to love boldly and unapologetically follow our passion

Contents

Acknowledgments

Everything we do with Ochsner Eat Fit is a collaborative affair, and this book is no different.

We are honored and grateful for the support of so many people and organizations who share our passion and support our mission to help members of our community live their strongest, healthiest lives.

A heartfelt thank-you for the teamwork and dedication of so many:

Our thousands of Alcohol Free For 40 participants over the years. Your journey and your trust inspired this book, and your experiences shaped its content.

Our Eat Fit partners, who nourish our bodies and spirits daily and so generously shared the recipes that inspired the drinks on these pages.

Ethan Skaggs, who planted the seed of an idea, the "what if" we create an Eat Fit-approved zero proof cocktail book. He dove in headfirst and became my coauthor in this project, bringing his cocktail expertise to life in these pages. Ethan's contributions to *Craft* also include photo editor and artist, as he provided the illustrations appearing throughout.

Melanie Warner Spencer, our executive editor and mentor throughout this project. You radiate enthusiasm and positivity, infusing such a spirit of fun into zero proof spirits.

Hope Frugé, our Eat Fit Monroe registered dietitian and photographer for *Craft,* for creating sophisticated and captivating images with an effortless ease and grace.

Savanna Latimer, our Eat Fit Baton Rouge registered dietitian and project manager for *Craft,* for your remarkable attention to detail and perseverance throughout, leading the charge in photoshoots, recipe analysis, editing, and proofreading—and serving as unofficial quality-control manager throughout the recipe-testing process.

Matt Vermeulen for generously giving your time, talents, and expertise in the cover design and the look and feel of the pages throughout *Craft*.

Our Eat Fit team, who helped select the recipes featured on these pages, reviewed copy, and put recipes to the test in the "real" world, including:

- Brittany Craft, Eat Fit Northshore registered dietitian, for analyzing, editing, and proofreading recipes with a striking level of precision and detail.
- Maria Sylvester Terry, Eat Fit NOLA registered dietitian and social media manager. Also recipe-tester coordinator, communication role model, and wordsmith extraordinaire.
- Yvette Perrier Quantz, Eat Fit Acadiana registered dietitian, recipe tester, and impressively efficient ingredient organizer.
- Anna Walter, Eat Fit Shreveport registered dietitian, recipe tester, and cheerleader.
- Erin Arceneaux, Eat Fit Program Coordinator, recipe tester, and our team's master planner.

Claire Hubley, Eat Fit Ambassador and production assistant, for organizing recipes and testers, sourcing ingredients, and serving as overall crisis solver, ensuring that our photoshoots ran as smoothly as possible.

Jeffrey Clark Style for lending us such glamorous vintage glassware. Your stunning array of crystal and glass, from gilded flutes to retro tumblers, added instant character and depth to the images on these pages.

The Chloe and Cavan in New Orleans, including chef John Bel, Robert LeBlanc, and the entire LeBlanc + Smith team, for your hospitality and generosity. Your chic and timeless spaces served as the perfect backdrops to photograph our drinks.

The Eli and Okaloosa in Monroe for sharing the intimate energy of your spaces—as well as the talented and delightful Hunter Heaslip to style our cocktails for our shoot on location in Monroe.

Recipe testers Ben McLauchlin, Phil and Christina de Gruy, Kristina Larson, Denise Morris, Susan Whelan, Melaina Ricks, Jenna Rae Vercillo, Joy Bruce, and Sarah Pitfield.

Simple-syrup testers Cole Newton, Elizabeth Pearce, Amy Davis, Claire Hubley, and Avni Gupta for sipping their way through seemingly endless batches of sweeteners and syrups.

The Pelican Publishing team for believing in this project, including Publisher Scott Campbell, Editor in Chief Nina Kooij, and Designer Cassie Zimmerman.

Ochsner Fitness Center dietitians Alexis Weilbaecher and Lauren Hulin for your enthusiastic support of all things Eat Fit.

Our leadership team at Ochsner Health and Ochsner Fitness Center: Diedra Dias, Wayne Morris, David Gaines, and Warner Thomas. Our Ochsner PR and marketing team, including Cheryl Jackson, Katie Fauquier, Melinda Daffin, Mimsie Ladner, and Sophia Gross. Thank you for believing in us and supporting us in what we love to do.

The Swerve & Whole Earth team for your guidance on creating the best simple syrups made with plant-based sweeteners.

Finally, a tremendous thank-you to all of our team's spouses and partners for supporting and sharing in this project. And most of all, I am grateful for the support and love of my husband, Brad. I love that you make me laugh until I can't breathe.

The Eat Fit Zero Proof Story

Why Zero Proof?

For starters, we like the way it sounds. A zero proof cocktail sounds and *feels* so much more sophisticated than a mocktail or a virgin cocktail. Also, we deserve flavorful drinks that rise above the typical interpretations of sugary, syrupy, juice-filled beverages. So, we prefer to go with *zero proof* cocktail.

Zero proof cocktails, with the flavors and complexity of traditional craft cocktails, are visually appealing, festive and fun, but still leave us feeling at the top of our game, no matter how many we may imbibe.

We're highly aware that a zero proof cocktail book coming out of booze-fueled New Orleans may seem a bit out of place. So, here's the backstory on how it came to be.

For most of my adult life, the concept of zero proof was something I never even thought about—it wasn't even a consideration. We're in New Orleans, after all, and drinking is such a part of our *laissez les bons temps rouler* way of life. Creating a zero proof cocktail book was the furthest thing from my mind.

Around the time I turned 40, I was looking for that edge—that extra bit of inspiration to dial back what was then a pretty steady routine of social drinking.

I was a columnist for the *New Orleans Times-Picayune* and pitched the idea to my editor: what if (two of my favorite words, by the way) we propose a post-Mardi Gras challenge to our fellow New Orleanians to go alcohol free for the 40 days of Lent—*and* encourage them to make it their own self-experiment by doing a series of labs and physical metrics, both before and after the challenge? I braced myself for a quick no, or at least a dubious eyebrow raise, from my editor. A bit to my surprise, she loved the concept.

I put myself through the challenge first. Quite frankly, I wasn't sure I would make it. Again—this is New Orleans. But it was important to me to experience firsthand the benefits I would soon be telling our readers they would experience. I also wanted to see just how quickly I might see results. If 40 days felt too daunting for some, what impact could they expect to see in as little as a week that might give them the motivation to hang in there?

After just one week, I was stunned by the benefits I was already seeing and feeling.

Situations that in the past elicited feelings of anxiety—heart racing, hands shaking, ears roaring—stayed the same, but my physical reactions to these stressors were all but gone. I slept more deeply, woke up more refreshed, and remembered my dreams more vividly. In just seven days, my liver enzymes and inflammatory markers were markedly lower (something that surprised even my primary care physician). I was sold.

It turns out—others were craving a similar experience as well. What started out as a citywide challenge quickly expanded to include participants around the world, joining in on the annual Alcohol Free For 40 challenge hosted by our Ochsner Eat Fit team.

The real-world experiences shared by our thousands of participants mirror what science is rapidly confirming—the whole-body benefits of going alcohol free are far reaching and, dare we say, life changing.

Some improvements can be measured objectively, such as blood pressure, triglycerides, liver enzymes, inflammatory markers, weight, and body fat. Other benefits, such as dealing with stress more effectively, improved sleep, more patience, and enhanced mental clarity, are also very real, and relevant markers of positive change beyond what is shown via ordinary lab tests.

Here's something I find wildly ironic: we often turn to alcohol to relieve stress. But while we're feeling all good and relaxed, sitting back and sipping our cocktail, the alcohol is actually revving up the stress responses in our brains. Our reactions to stress the following day feel even more intense than before—in some instances even leading to full-blown panic attacks. Unfortunately, it's all too easy to slip into the habit of turning to alcohol as a shortcut to unwind and decompress, fueling that vicious cycle of our body's heightened stress response.

Another little-discussed topic—and one of the hard truths that can be tough to accept—is the influence of alcohol on cancer. It's a known carcinogen, raising our risk for esophageal, liver, gastric, bile duct, and breast cancer. The breast cancer stats are shocking: a large-scale review of more than 50 studies found that a woman's risk of breast cancer goes up 7 percent for each drink consumed per day. For women who have two to three alcoholic drinks per day, their breast cancer risk is 20 percent higher.

Meanwhile, since the scientific community is discovering that pretty much everything comes down to the gut, we can't *not* mention alcohol's impact on gastrointestinal health. A balanced, healthy gut microbiome is essential, affecting everything from our mood to our weight to our bathroom habits. There's little debate that alcohol is one of the strongest microbiome disruptors that leads to imbalanced, unhappy gut microbes.

So as our Alcohol Free For 40 participants started to experience these benefits for themselves, the movement gained traction.

Participants came back year after year, with the Alcohol Free For 40 challenge serving as their annual reset, recalibrating their relationship with alcohol. Some have decided to continue the zero proof lifestyle well beyond the challenge.

That's how our editor, Melanie Warner Spencer, happened into this project. An award-winning lifestyle journalist and photographer based in New Orleans, she made the decision to take a yearlong break from alcohol after her experience with Alcohol Free For 40. Melanie infuses a party into everything she does, and her zero proof lifestyle is no exception. She is well versed in the vast array of zero proof spirits and wines, serving as my go-to resource for all things zero proof craft cocktails.

Why Eat Fit?

Zero proof alone doesn't make a drink "good" for us. It's not just about the alcohol content (we have plenty of Eat Fit-approved cocktails made with full-proof spirits). Sure, the amount of alcohol matters, but it's just one element.

One common limitation of alcohol-free drinks is the slow creep of added sugar, typically in the form of spirits replacers, alcohol-free wines and beers, or mixers and syrups.

Our Ochsner Eat Fit team of registered dietitians has worked with dozens of bartenders to create innovative craft cocktails that are zero proof *and* no added sugar. Our nutritional criteria limit even 100 percent fruit juice to one ounce, with no sugary syrups or mixers. Calories, carbs, and sugars are kept in check, while flavor and creativity prevail.

Enter Ethan Skaggs—this book was actually his idea. A graduate of the University of Pennsylvania with dual degrees in architecture and art history, Ethan's eye for design is evident in the bar programs he's designed for various New Orleans restaurants, most recently Gris-Gris, an Eat Fit partner. We knew we could always count on Ethan for enthusiastic renditions of both traditional and craft cocktails. So, when he asked if I wanted to collaborate on a book filled with cocktails that were both zero proof *and* Eat Fit, the answer was an easy and enthusiastic *yes*.

That is the story of how these people who live in a festive, booze-infused city like New Orleans have come together to bring you *Craft: The Eat Fit Guide to Zero Proof Cocktails*.

Navigating the Zero Proof World

Zero proof is not an all or nothing proposition. It's about choice and drinking mindfully. This book—and the entire concept of mindful drinking—is designed to provide inspiration and guidance not only to people who aren't drinking, but also to those who are. You may choose to go entirely alcohol free, take a break, or simply avoid alcohol during the week. This book can be your reference tool when friends come to your home and they aren't drinking for whatever reason that day, that week, or simply in that moment. Or you may be like my stepmom Pat, eager to try these gorgeous, low-sugar drinks and looking forward to experimenting by swapping zero proof spirits for the real thing. If ingredients with trace amounts of alcohol or products that mimic alcoholic beverages are a trigger for you, it's best to just avoid the recipes that include those items.

How to Do the Alcohol Free For 40 Challenge on Your Own

Of all the wellness-centered initiatives I've been involved with over the past couple of decades, Alcohol Free For 40 is quite possibly the most rewarding. But you don't have to wait for next year's post-Mardi Gras challenge to get started.

You can take the Alcohol Free For 40 challenge any time of year. Simply select a window of time—it can be 40 days, but if that feels like too much, it can be two weeks, 10 days, or one week. Determine what feels manageable, yet still like a "challenge" for you.

Enlist a friend, or multiple friends, to join you. Be mindful of who you bring into your alcohol-free circle, though. The team approach can be a powerful motivator, but it can also make it feel a lot easier to throw in the towel or have "just one" drink if others are, as well. You'll find year-round social support at our Alcohol Free For 40 Facebook Group and other online forums such as Melanie's Drink Fit Club.

Above all, go into it with an open mind. You'll likely start out with one set of expectations, what you hope to see and feel, but you may experience the strongest benefits in other, completely different aspects of your mind, body, and spirit.

Establish as many of your pre-challenge metrics as possible (see below), *before* you start. Repeat these at the end of your alcohol-free challenge. Your physician can place the lab orders, and the lab results will have the normal ranges listed for your reference.

Physical Markers

Weight
Blood pressure
Body composition via body fat scale, such as InBody or Tanita
Close-up photo of face (and we mean *uncomfortably* close, so you can really see the detail of your eyes and skin)

Lab Markers

CMP (comprehensive metabolic panel; includes liver markers AST, ALT, and alkaline phosphatase)
Lipid Panel (includes triglycerides, which can be affected by alcohol)
GGT (a specific liver test that's most affected by alcohol)
Vitamin B12
Folate
hs-CRP (marker of inflammation)
ESR (marker of inflammation)

Bringing the Party

Our approach to zero proofing it is all about layering in a spirit of celebration and curiosity. Alcohol-free cocktails can still be just as festive and fun—and in some cases, even *more* fun.

It can feel strange at first, even a bit scary, to even think about not drinking socially, especially if we haven't done it in a while, or ever. It's easy to turn to alcohol as a confidence booster in social settings, but there can be a heck of a lot of reward when we're *not* drinking. Realizing that we can still have fun, and still *be* fun—even without alcohol—is liberating.

It's also a fantastic opportunity to share your zero proof cocktail creations with friends and family. We never know where someone's coming from, what place they're in, especially as it relates to drinking. Simply normalizing the concept of zero proof drinking, and providing unspoken encouragement to perhaps just give it a try, can be incredibly impactful.

We can't emphasize it enough—just have fun with it. You can follow these recipes verbatim or use them as a starting point and experiment with different flavors and infusions to add your own personal spin. There's no right or wrong, only limitless potential.

Crafting the Zero Proof Cocktail

Preparing a sophisticated and flavorful cocktail, zero proof or otherwise, is simple yet can feel daunting. Ever since the craft-cocktail revolution swept the country in the late '90s, there has been a sense of pressure to create the "perfect" cocktail, with at-home mixologists striving to master just the right blend of palate, harmony, patience, and imagination to create a balanced libation.

Fortunately, things have loosened up over the past 20 years. Crafting cocktails is now about experimentation and self-expression, bending the traditionally stringent rules to infuse a strong element of creativity and personality into drinks.

We believe that the only "tools" necessary to create a successful drink are perseverance, attention to detail, and a spirit of adventure. This book is your guide to sparking craft-cocktail creativity. Take note of the flavor profiles you gravitate toward as you work your way through our curated ingredients, recipes, and pro tips to develop your own personal drink style.

Practically speaking, there are a few tangible items to consider when navigating the Eat Fit zero proof world, the first being the base ingredients that make up the foundation of your drink. Not only are we looking for ingredients that are alcohol free, but we also want these ingredients to be free of added sugars, artificial sweeteners, and colors.

Depending on the drink, we may or may not be using one of the many varieties of zero proof spirits available on the market. Then there's the choice of mixers, sweeteners, or flavor enhancers such as bitters, herbs, or spices.

Finally, how will we style this drink? Our choice of glassware and garnish can be almost as important as nailing that just-right combination of ingredients. In fact, Ethan recommends selecting glassware *before* we start building our zero proof cocktail, since it influences the volume we have to work with. Of course, garnish, while integral to the sensory experience, adds more than just color and beauty—it also releases aromatics, oils, and, ultimately, flavor.

We know. The idea of creating this exquisite balance and breadth with a seemingly infinite list of potential ingredients can be overwhelming. Don't worry; we've got you covered. We provide fundamental parameters to narrow the scope, keeping the focus on an array of Eat Fit-approved ingredients that allow for ample creativity. We'll walk you through each step, whether you're designing your own zero proof cocktails, adapting traditional favorites to be zero proof, or simply recreating the recipes on these pages. This goes for seasoned zero proof pros as well as those just dipping a toe into the zero proof space. We're here to support your adventure.

Craft Zero Proof Toolkit

Consider this your step-by-step guide to building the perfect zero proof cocktail.

Base Ingredients

These are the foundation of the drink, typically providing the bulk of the drink's volume. Our choice of these ingredients matters, as they serve to balance and elevate your cocktail experience. As always, we're looking for all-natural options with little or no sugary carbs.

- **Sparkling Water.** Whether it's your favorite sparkling mineral water (Topo Chico is my personal favorite; it's just so bubbly, and the carbonation sticks around for hours) or club soda, this no-sugar spritz adds volume and effervescence. We recommend steering clear of tonic water, however, since it packs in as much sugar as a soft drink—and diet tonic typically is artificially sweetened. If you want the quinine alkalinity of tonic water, try a brand like Zevia, naturally sweetened with stevia.

- **Kombucha.** An ale-like sweet-yet-sour carbonated beverage made from black or green teas, kombucha is a top source of probiotics. Because kombucha is made by fermenting tea with yeast and friendly bacteria, it does have trace amounts of alcohol. For a lot of people it's a non-issue, as commercially available kombucha contains less than 0.5 percent alcohol. Keep this in mind if you avoid products containing any amount of alcohol.

- **Herbal Tea.** We love reaping the many health benefits of green and black tea, and herbal tea is an easy way to slip a variety of flavors—and volume—into your cocktail. House favorites include hibiscus, orange blossom, peach oolong, blueberry, and passionfruit, but you really can't go wrong. Play around with your favorites, mixing and matching flavor profiles in our tea-based cocktails.

- **Fruit Juice.** You'll see 100 percent fruit juice in many of our recipes, though not more than 1 ounce per drink, to keep sugars (yes, even natural sugars) in check.

Sweeteners + Syrups

By "sweeteners and syrups," we mean zero-sugar sweeteners and syrups, of course. No artificial sweeteners for us—we prefer to keep things natural with plant-based sweeteners. Here's a summary of our favorites; we go deeper in our chapter "The Art + Science of Sweeteners + Simple Syrups" on page 31.

- **Allulose.** The most neutral of the plant-based sweeteners, allulose performs the best in simple syrups, meaning it stays in suspension without recrystallizing or settling out. Making your own allulose simple syrup is easy (see page 39), or you can buy a premade version (Allulose Syrup by Wholesome Sweetener is our favorite brand).

- **Swerve.** Neutral in flavor and slightly sweeter than allulose, granular Swerve works spectacularly for rimming a glass, muddling into berries, or blending into a frozen drink. Swerve can also be used to create a simple syrup, though it tends to recrystallize easily (just heat it a bit and you're back in business).

- **Swerve Brown Sugar.** If you hold this brown sugar replacer in your hand, it has the same structure and feel as "real" brown sugar. Not only is it perfect for a hot toddy or zero proof coffee-based cocktail, it is our top choice for stellar baked goods. There is no bitter aftertaste and it measures cup for cup like sugar in your favorite recipes.

- **Swoon.** We've tried a variety of DIY and ready-made monk fruit-sweetened simple syrups, and Swoon is our top pick, hands down. Swoon adds a silky texture and natural sweetness to cocktails. Just keep in mind that it's intensely sweet—a little goes a long way.

Bitters

Highly concentrated infusions of botanicals, bitters add a certain *je ne sais quoi* that makes any drink feel more like a true cocktail. In our "DIY Infusions" chapter, we guide you through the steps to make your own bitters, along with a few brands we recommend (page 47).

Fresh Herbs

Dried, muddled, infused into tea or syrups, or used for aromatics and garnish, fresh herbs are essential for classics and craft cocktails alike.

- Must-haves include mint, basil, rosemary, thyme, and sage.
- Are you feeling a little creative? We recommend experimenting with dill, shiso, tarragon, cilantro, lemon verbena, and oregano.

Barware

Shaker Tin. Functional and dramatic, shaking a cocktail immediately makes us feel like a real bartender. Two common styles are the **Boston shaker** (two pieces) and the **Cobbler shaker** (three pieces with built-in strainer).

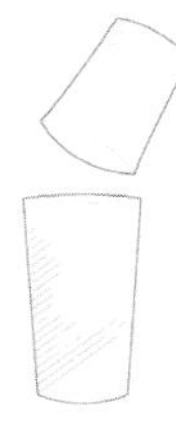

The Boston is what you've likely seen most bartenders use, the style that can be shaken with one hand. The original concept for this shaker actually uses a pint glass as one half of the shaker, though now most come with two metal pieces.

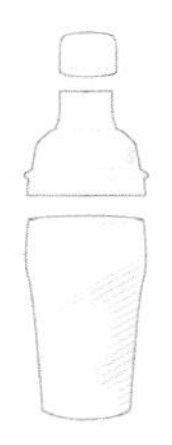

With the Cobbler, it's important to note that it holds a smaller volume and pours a bit slower—and from time to time the shaker might be difficult to separate, as the metal chills and contracts.

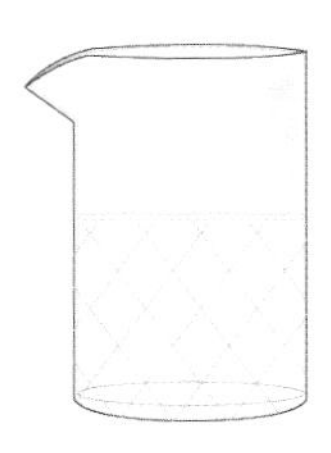

For cocktails that are best stirred versus shaken, the **Yarai mixing glass** is the professional bartender's mixing vessel of choice. Using a clear glass instead of a metal shaker allows us to stir the drink with accuracy, ensuring the correct color and consistency with just a glance.

Shake or Stir/

It depends on the ingredients—and personal preference. The general rule is that we stir spirit-only drinks and we shake cocktails that contain juices, creams, or other mixers. Essentially, shake ingredients that might separate.

Muddler. This is your tool for smashing, mashing, and mixing ingredients to express and incorporate the oils, juices, and aromatics prior to adding liquid ingredients.

Bar Spoon. Though desperate times may have you considering using a butter knife to mix your cocktails, a bar spoon has several applications. One measured bar spoon is equal to 1 teaspoon, and its long handle reaches the bottom of the tallest of tumblers, allowing you to mix ingredients directly in a glass or vessel.

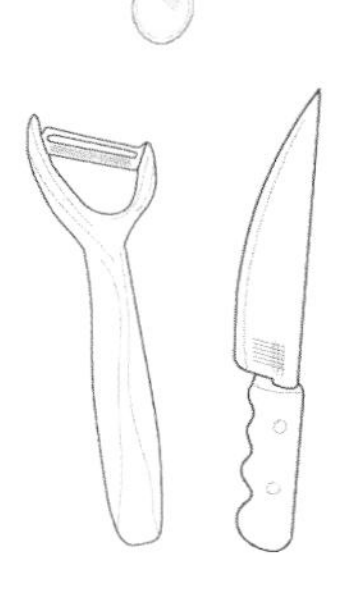

Peeler and Knife. From peeling fruit skins into swaths to cutting whole fruit into wedges or wheels, these tools give you the most control in creating exquisite garnishes.

- Ethan recommends the **Y peeler** specifically. With a blade that's perpendicular to the handle, it's shaped like and handles like a razor. This provides a thinner cut of fruit and vegetable skin than other types of peelers, leaving more of the rind and pulp behind.

- The **channel knife** makes it possible to shape produce peels into spirals and twists. Be patient, though—it can take plenty of practice to make perfect peels.

- A **paring knife** gives solid control in creating the most precise cuts.

Strainer. Once you shake, there are two types of strainers you may need:

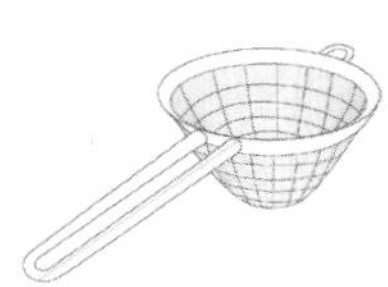

- **A fine-mesh strainer** is essential for every home bar, even if you're using a Cobbler shaker that has a built-in strainer. The mesh strainer is used to double strain a drink, ensuring that ice chips and other ingredient remnants don't end up in our cocktail.

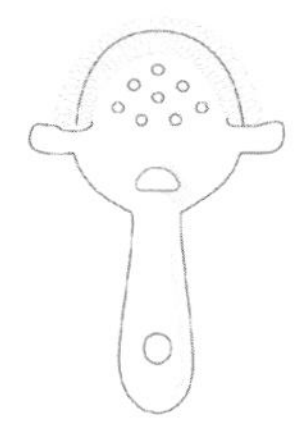

- The **Hawthorne strainer** is a two- (or four-) pronged strainer (some are built into the shaker tin; others are a separate little gadget) that uses metal coils to easily separate your liquid from ice, herbs, and other ingredients.

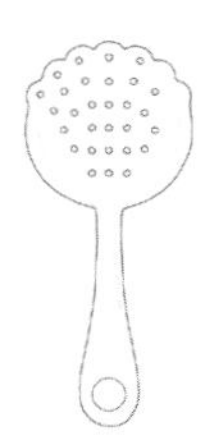

- The **Julep strainer**, which looks like a small colander with a handle, is perfectly suited for the Yarai mixing glass.

The Art + Science of Sweeteners + Simple Syrups

Sugar is the nutritional downfall of many a cocktail, zero proof or otherwise.

From simple syrups and sweeteners to sugary mixers and juices, these added sugars have the potential to be more detrimental than we may realize. Beyond calories and weight gain, added sugars contribute to whole-body inflammation and can set us on a blood-sugar rollercoaster, causing and perpetuating cravings for more carbs and more sugars.

Fortunately, we have ample options for naturally low- and no-sugar varieties of pretty much any ingredient that might be featured in a cocktail.

There's a lot happening lately in the world of better-for-you simple syrups, specifically those centered on natural, plant-based, zero-sugar sweeteners, making it easier than ever to effortlessly dial back on sugary carbs.

The Role of Simple Syrups

The strategic use of sweeteners is essential in creating a balanced cocktail.

Traditionally made with a one-to-one ratio of sugar to water, simple syrups work particularly well for sweetening chilled beverages—much better than stirring a granular sweetener into cold liquid and crossing our fingers that it dissolves. Spoiler alert: it doesn't.

Simple syrups are just sugar water, though, packing a quick 80 calories and 20 grams of added sugar into every ounce.

Forget everything you know about sugar-free ingredients. For years, the main sweeteners used in sugar-free simple syrups were artificial sweeteners such as aspartame (Equal) and sucralose (Splenda), both of which have a synthetic flavor and sharp aftertaste.

Zero-calorie sweeteners have come a long way, and the array of plant-based sweeteners now available has made it a cinch to replicate the flavor, sweetness, and mouthfeel of traditional simple syrups.

Natural Plant-Based Sweeteners

Plant-based sweeteners can be divided into two main categories: high intensity and low intensity. Each of our recipes has been designed to include a specific sweetener; sweeteners are not interchangeable between these two categories, at least not easily.

High-intensity sweeteners are as much as 400 times sweeter than table sugar and include products like stevia and monk fruit.

- **Stevia,** commonly available in liquid or granular form, is approximately 150 to 200 times sweeter than sugar. Its intense sweetness can actually be perceived as bitter, so many of the granular stevia products on shelves are actually a blend of stevia along with erythritol or monk fruit.

- **Monk fruit**, also referred to as *lo han guo,* is roughly 200 times sweeter than sugar. Extracted from a fruit that has been consumed in Southern China for centuries, monk fruit is said to be named after the Buddhist monks who grew the fruit more than 800 years ago. Monk fruit is available in granular form as well as pre-made simple syrups.

Low-intensity sweeteners (70 to 100 percent of the sweetness of sugar) include allulose and erythritol. There are others, such as xylitol and maltitol, but they tend to have unwanted side effects like GI distress (and nobody wants that).

- **Allulose** is approximately 70 percent as sweet as sugar. It's not zero-calorie, but with only 0.4 calories per gram (compared to 4 calories per gram of sugar), it's close. Compared to erythritol, allulose caramelizes and browns more like sugar. It also has the most neutral flavor of all of the plant-based sweeteners. Allulose is available in granular form as well as a premade syrup.

- **Erythritol** is also roughly 70 percent as sweet as sugar. Small amounts of erythritol are found naturally in fruits; most erythritol is produced by fermenting glucose with various yeasts. It's a bulky sweetener, providing a volume similar to that of sugar, so it's often combined with high-intensity plant-based sweeteners.

- **Swerve** brand sweetener is a blend of erythritol and prebiotic fibers. It's sweeter than erythritol, closer to a one-to-one ratio with sugar. The prebiotic fibers contribute to this sweetness and help Swerve to brown and caramelize more like real sugar.

Zero-Sugar Simple Syrups

When it comes to making our own Eat Fit simple syrups, our preference is to stick with low-intensity sweeteners, namely Swerve and allulose, as they come the closest to mimicking the flavor and sweetness of a traditional simple syrup.

Though they're both classified as low-intensity sweeteners, there's still a significant bit of variation between the two in terms of flavor, sweetness, and how they behave when heated and dissolved to make a simple syrup.

Simple syrup made with allulose, for example, has a neutral flavor and a mild sweetness with subtle notes of honey and vanilla. The granular allulose stays in suspension incredibly well, meaning that it doesn't recrystallize or settle to the bottom, even when refrigerated. Our Eat Fit Simple Syrup recipe using allulose has a satisfying viscosity, somewhere between nectar and honey.

Swerve-sweetened simple syrup, on the other hand, is a notch sweeter than allulose syrup, with a flavor, intensity, and sweetness profile that's more like traditional sugar-sweetened simple syrup. It has a thinner consistency than allulose syrup and tends to recrystallize relatively quickly, due in part to Swerve's prebiotic fibers.

This isn't an issue if we're preparing and using the simple syrup immediately. But for those looking to make a batch of Eat Fit Simple Syrup to use over the course of a few days or weeks, it can be a hassle to have to continually reheat the Swerve-sweetened simple syrup to coax the crystals back into solution.

In spite of the nuances in flavor and sweetness, mixing and matching Swerve- or allulose-sweetened simple syrups across different recipes typically works fine. Just keep in mind that the ratio of sweetener to water varies, as noted in the chart that follows.

High-intensity sweeteners such as monk fruit and stevia don't work as well in simple syrups, especially not DIY simple syrups. There are a few store-bought brands that we like; these typically contain additional ingredients, however (think gums and lactic acid), to boost the quality of the finished product.

A little goes a long way, as both monk fruit- and stevia-sweetened simple syrups are so intensely sweet—almost cloyingly sweet—and can easily be perceived as bitter. Interestingly, we've found that people who typically like artificial sweeteners (think aspartame, sucralose [Splenda], or saccharin) tend to gravitate toward syrups made with these high-intensity sweeteners. Monk-fruit simple syrup is also popular among our Eat Fit bartenders, who artfully layer it into the flavors and complexity of their drinks.

We've created this reference chart for Eat Fit simple syrups to help guide you in replicating the true essence of simple syrups.

Plant-Based Sweeteners Reference

	Erythritol	Allulose
Sweetness compared to sugar	60-70%	70%
Simple syrup ratio (water to sweetener)	1 part water to 0.5 part sweetener	1 part water to 1.5 parts sweetener
Sweetness notes	Mild	Medium
Flavor + aroma notes	Neutral	Undertones of honey, vanilla
Viscosity notes	Similar to traditional simple syrup	Between nectar and honey
[Notes]	We love it for baking – less for our drinks	This is our favorite all-around for DIY simple syrups. Stays in suspensio even when fridge

Swerve	Stevia	Monk Fruit
100%	150-200x	200x
1 part to 0.5 part sweetener	DIY not recommended	DIY not recommended
Most like traditional sugar	Intense	Intense
Neutral	Can be perceived as bitter	Can be perceived as bitter. Strong, pungent aroma
Similar to traditional simple syrup	Thin, watery	Thin, watery
Imparts an interesting cooling effect. Crystalizes when refrigerated	Not recommended for drinks	Brings a slight bitterness along with the sweetness

Eat Fit Simple Syrup

Makes approximately 1 cup

1 cup water

½ cup Swerve granular or 1½ cups granular allulose

In a saucepan, bring water to a boil. Reduce to medium-high heat and add sweetener. Stir to dissolve and continue to heat for 10 minutes. Pour into heat-safe glass container and refrigerate to chill. Store unused portion in airtight container in refrigerator for up to 4 weeks.

Rosemary Simple Syrup

Makes approximately 1 cup

1 cup water

½ cup Swerve granular or 1½ cups granular allulose

½ cup loosely packed rosemary sprigs

In a small saucepan, bring water to a boil. Reduce to medium-high heat and add sweetener. Stir to dissolve and continue to heat for 10 minutes. Add rosemary sprigs. Transfer to heat-safe glass container and allow to infuse for at least 1 hour. Double strain before using. Refrigerate unused portion in a sealed airtight container for up to 4 weeks.

Ginger Simple Syrup

Makes approximately 1 cup

1 cup water

1 tablespoon coarsely grated gingerroot (approximately 1 knob)

½ cup Swerve granular or 1½ cups granular allulose

In a small saucepan, bring water and ginger to a boil. Reduce to medium-high heat and add sweetener. Stir to dissolve and continue to heat for 10 minutes. Transfer to heat-safe glass container and allow to infuse for at least 1 hour. Double strain before using. Refrigerate unused portion in a sealed airtight container for up to 4 weeks.

Raspberry Simple Syrup

Makes approximately 1 cup

½ cup Swerve granular

1 cup fresh raspberries

1 cup water

Add Swerve and raspberries to a zip-top bag and roll with rolling pin until lightly crushed. In a saucepan, bring water to a boil. Reduce to medium-high heat, add Swerve-raspberry mixture, and stir to dissolve. Remove from heat and set aside for 10 minutes. Double strain into heat-safe container and refrigerate for at least 1 hour. Refrigerate unused portion in a sealed airtight container for up to 4 weeks.

Oleo Saccharum

Makes approximately ¼ cup

1 cup orange peels (from approximately 3 oranges)

Zest of 2 oranges

⅓ cup granular allulose

Juice of 1 orange

In a medium mixing bowl, combine orange peels, orange zest, and allulose. Muddle every few minutes for approximately 15 minutes. Top with juice and muddle periodically for another 15 minutes. Double strain before using. Refrigerate unused portion in a sealed airtight container for up to 4 weeks.

Time Saver /

Try this shortcut if you don't have the time (or patience) to make the real thing: replace each tablespoon of Oleo Saccharum in a recipe with 2 teaspoons simple syrup, 1 teaspoon orange juice, and 1 pinch orange zest.

DIY Infusions: Bitters, Shrubs + Simple Syrups

It's especially satisfying to create a drink—or anything, for that matter—using ingredients made from scratch.

If you're feeling creative, experiment with handcrafting your own infusions, including bitters, shrubs, and Eat Fit simple syrups. While each can be purchased in stores or online, making our own allows us to experiment with unusual ingredients and custom flavor combinations.

Before getting into the specifics of each, become familiar with and learn to understand the differences among these common cocktail ingredients.

- **Bitters** are distilled botanicals. They're extremely concentrated; only a few drops are added to a cocktail. Many, but not all, contain trace amounts of alcohol.

- **Shrubs** are a blend of vinegar with fruit. Only a small amount—a quarter- or half-ounce or so—is typically added per drink.

- **Simple syrup** is the simplest of the three. Traditionally made with equal parts water and sugar, simple syrup works particularly well as a sweetener in drink recipes. Our Eat Fit simple syrups (see "The Art + Science of Sweeteners + Simple Syrups" chapter) use natural plant-based sweeteners that still function like simple syrup, without the calories, carbs, or sugars.

Each of these techniques is centered on infusion, the process of extracting an ingredient's flavor into liquid. Any liquid can be infused—water, oil, vinegar, syrup, spirits, even zero proof spirits.

Whatever we happen to be infusing, a few key strategies are helpful. Keep in mind, for example, that increasing the exposed surface area of ingredients (think chopped herbs versus whole) increases the rate of infusion.

Be patient and consider making notes as you go. Different ingredients yield different results, but it's important to note that even the *same* ingredients, when used in varying climates or circumstances, can behave uniquely. Jotting notes about ingredient measurements and environment helps to ensure consistency when replicating your recipe.

Once you master your favorite infusion, make a batch of it to keep on hand. While we love these in zero proof cocktail recipes, even just adding a bit of bitters, shrubs, or syrups to sparkling water creates the feel of a zero proof cocktail, instantly and effortlessly.

Bitters

A distilled blend of botanicals, bitters are highly concentrated infusions that add that special *something* to any drink. To get a sense of what we're talking about, add a few drops to sparkling water to see and taste the difference.

Originally created for medicinal purposes, most varieties of bitters technically have a high percentage of alcohol by volume (ABV). They're so ultra-potent, however, that we need only a few drops (or dashes) to have a tremendous impact on the aromatics and flavor profile of a cocktail. The amount of alcohol contributed by these few drops is so minimal that it is considered to be insignificant. For those who have decided to avoid even trace amounts of alcohol, however, it may be best to find readymade alcohol-free bitters (read on for our brand suggestions) or use our zero proof DIY bitters recipe, below.

Making our own bitters can be quite rewarding, giving us the opportunity to experiment with limitless permutations of flavors and elements that influence the end product.

There are three main categories of ingredients to consider when creating your own zero proof bitters: bittering agents, aromatics, and vegetable glycerin. (Traditional bitters are made with grain alcohol, but glycerin is a surprisingly appropriate replacement.)

The most common bittering agents include dandelion, valerian, licorice, and burdock roots. We also recommend considering a dried bark, such as sarsaparilla or wild cherry bark. These components stay true to their name, as their purpose is to provide a bitter base, and when used alone, they result in the earthy qualities that we expect from bitters.

Aromatics are a little more of a free-for-all. Think anything that provides a strong scent when macerated, whether it be through an oil, spice, herb, flower, or dried fruit. These aromatics not only add flavor but also serve to round out the bitters.

For the beginner bitters brewer, we recommend aromatics such as citrus peels (orange, lime, lemon, grapefruit, to start with); roots, herbs, and flowers (ginger, mint, rosemary, sage, chamomile, hibiscus, lavender, lemongrass, thyme are our favorites); and spices (such as allspice, aniseed, cardamom, cloves, fennel seed, nutmeg, peppercorn). As you get more adventurous, try adding toasted nuts; dried fruits like cherries, figs, or raisins; or beans like cacao or coffee.

Finally, vegetable glycerin is the glue that breaks down and subsequently binds your bittering agents and aromatics into the final mixture. Since ingredients reach peak infusion at different rates, we recommend creating a separate infusion for each bittering agent or aromatic (collectively referred to as your botanicals), then blending these to create the final product.

DIY Bitters

Place each botanical in its own clear jar, clearly labeled with the botanical name and date. For faster infusions, we recommend chopping, crushing, or cracking ingredients—this gives a greater surface area, which speeds infusion rate.

Pour the vegetable glycerin into each jar, ensuring all parts of the botanicals are submerged. Cover tightly to prevent any exposure to oxygen. Throughout the infusion process, shake each of the jars daily.

This is where things really get fun. After the first day, you can begin to smell and sample the tinctures to assess progress. While there's not a scientific way to determine the readiness of your infusion—it's really personal preference—we do have a couple of tips.

Place a couple drops of each infusion in your palm and rub your hands together to smell. To sample by tasting, add a couple of drops to a small glass (roughly 8 ounces) of sparkling or still water. You'll know that your infusion is ready when your palate can detect (meaning you can start to taste and smell) the expression of the original ingredient.

When you've determined each tincture is complete, strain the flavoring ingredients out of each jar. Because we don't want any solids in the final product, a fine strainer or even a coffee filter works best.

The most important step of the process is blending, similar to how a winemaker makes wine. Once each of the botanicals is infused and strained, use a dropper or pipette to start adding each one to a glass jar or small bottle, to create a new mixture. Don't forget to take notes of your measurements. Sample your blend as you go, though keep in mind that it can take days or weeks for the flavors to fully incorporate. Bitters made with vegetable glycerin can be stored in the refrigerator for up to two months.

We encourage you to experiment with your own blends, mixing and matching flavor profiles that you enjoy. To provide a bit of inspiration, here are a few of Ethan's favorite blends.

- **Orange Bitters:** 14 parts orange peel, 3 parts cardamom pods, 2 parts coriander, 1 part vanilla bean, 1 part whole clove

- **Rhubarb Bitters:** 10 parts rhubarb, 4 parts lime, 4 parts dried juniper berries, 1 part chamomile, 1 part fennel seed

- **Lavender and Lemongrass Bitters:** 14 parts lavender, 12 parts lemongrass, 6 parts orange peel, 3 parts vanilla bean, 1 part gingerroot, 1 part whole allspice

- **Chocolate Bitters:** 12 parts cocoa nibs, 6 parts cardamom pods, 4 parts cinnamon stick, 3 parts wild cherry bark, 2 parts sarsaparilla bark, 2 parts vanilla bean

Readymade Bitters

If the DIY approach feels like too much, there are plenty of options for purchasing bitters:

Angostura is the most widely used aromatic bitters, imparting a spiciness with notes of clove and cinnamon. Originating in Venezuela and now produced in Trinidad and Tobago, these bitters are vital to creating the perfect Old Fashioned, Manhattan, Champagne Cocktail, and other classics. Like many of their kind, these were first developed for medicinal purposes—specifically for aid in digestion.

Peychaud's, a New Orleans staple, provides a sweeter, cherry take on clove and nutmeg. We do want to note that Peychaud's contains red 40, an artificial food dye that we typically recommend steering clear of. In this case, we opted to include Peychaud's for two main reasons (beyond its New Orleans connection—it was created in the Crescent City in the 1800s): there is not another bitters on the market that brings the same flavor to a drink, and recipes literally call for drops, resulting in a tiny, miniscule, close-to-nonexistent amount of red 40 per serving.

El Guapo is a New Orleans-based, woman-owned company that produces a continually evolving line of intriguing varieties, such as *Love Potion #9 Lavender* and *Polynesian Kiss,* and the regionally inspired *Chicory Pecan* and *Crawfish Boil Bitters.* They are also one of few brands of bitters that are 100 percent zero proof.

Shrubs

In the drink world, a shrub—also referred to as a drinking vinegar—is a concentrated syrup of fruit, sugar, and vinegar. It's incredibly versatile (nearly any fruit can be used in a shrub) and efficient (unlike bitters, making a shrub only takes about 20 minutes).

While premade shrubs or drinking vinegars are available, homemade shrubs are inexpensive and allow us to explore a vast array of flavor possibilities to create custom drinks.

To keep shrubs Eat Fit approved, we recommend using our Eat Fit Simple Syrup (see page 39). Use equal parts Eat Fit Simple Syrup, sliced fruit, and vinegar. Red wine vinegar is Ethan's preference, though you can also use apple cider vinegar, traditional balsamic vinegar, or champagne vinegar.

Wine-based vinegars, including red wine, white wine, and balsamic vinegar, do contain trace amounts of alcohol. It's a negligible amount for all practical purposes—though for some it may be worth noting that a tablespoon of wine vinegar may contain the equivalent of a drop of ethanol.

DIY Shrub

In a medium saucepan, bring Eat Fit Simple Syrup to a low simmer. Add sliced or slightly mashed fruit. While stirring, start to lightly muddle the fruit in the pan. Adding 1 or 2 sprigs of a fresh herb such as rosemary, mint, or basil will add more depth. Stir continuously until the fruit has softened and incorporated into the syrup. Add vinegar and stir for about 1 minute. Remove from heat and let sit for 3 to 4 minutes. Using a mesh strainer, pour into a heat-safe glass jar and store in the refrigerator for up to 4 weeks.

Syrups

Simple syrup is the easiest of the three infusions. A plain simple syrup is equal parts water and sugar, cooked down into a clear syrup. It serves as a sweetener that can be used in any recipe that calls for sugar.

Several natural plant-based, zero-sugar simple syrups are available in stores or online. Two of our favorites are Allulose Syrup by Wholesome brand and Swoon's monk fruit simple syrup.

Our DIY Eat Fit simple syrups use plant-based sweeteners; we prefer either allulose or Swerve. But even the most basic simple syrup provides the opportunity to showcase your creativity. The process of creating the syrup is an infusion in itself, and we can take it a step further by infusing these Eat Fit simple syrups with pretty much any type of herb, spice, or fruit. For simple syrup recipes, go to page 39.

Glassware

Even the most well balanced cocktail isn't fully dressed without a proper glass. Like our own choice of outfit for the day or occasion, our selection of glassware can elevate a drink's expression and impression, even influencing factors like drinkability and taste. While there are countless varieties of specialty glassware from around the world, we've narrowed it down to the eight most relevant and useful for at-home use. Understanding the sometimes-subtle differences among these glassware options will help guide you as you select the style and presentation for your zero proof masterpiece.

Martini

Quite possibly the most iconic on the list, the martini glass (also referred to as a cocktail glass) is intended for drinks served *up*, meaning without ice. The wide, open mouth of the glass is designed to release a drink's natural aromatics and, of course, convey a sense of elegance. Lift from the stem, pinky optional.

Coupe

Similar in style to the classic martini glass, the coupe has a broad, shallow bowl and holds a slightly smaller volume of liquid. Recognized as the original champagne vessel—and one of the first official cocktail glasses—the coupe is typically used for frothier beverages containing fruit juices or egg whites. You may have noticed many craft cocktail bars have returned to the traditional coupe in place of the martini glass. No need to get all fancy—it's simply pronounced "coop," not "coo-pay."

Flute

This classic is pretty straightforward, as it continues to reign supreme as the ultimate sparkling-wine glass, as well as the vessel of choice for any cocktail filled with bubbly.

Highball + Collins

Often used interchangeably, both are tall, cylindrical glasses intended for drinks served over ice. This shape works well for muddling and for preserving the carbonation of sparkling drinks. Highball glasses typically hold 8 to 12 ounces, while Collins glasses are slightly larger, up to 14 ounces.

Rocks

Also referred to as an old fashioned glass, or a lowball glass, a rocks glass is best suited for classics or for serving straight liquors on the rocks or neat, without ice. Many faceted rocks glasses have a nearly invisible notch right at the 2-ounce mark, signifying a standard pour when serving liquor neat.

Wine

The white-wine glass on the left could also be called a *uni* (uniform) glass, and it is taller and narrower than a red-wine glass. A perfect pour for either is just below the widest part of the glass, typically 5 ounces. Red-wine glasses tend to be larger and more bowl like, allowing for proper aeration, which helps to smooth tannins that are often perceived as bitter.

Snifter

The broader base provides a larger surface area, allowing for full expression of aromatics, while the narrow top serves to contain these notes within the glass. The bottom of the glass is rounded so it can be cupped in the hand, adding natural warmth to the liquor or liqueur and allowing the full experience of nose, palate, finish.

Hurricane

Contrary to popular belief, this glass isn't named after the popular drink at New Orleans' famed Pat O'Brien's. It is actually named after a hurricane lamp, which got its moniker from the glass shade's ability to prevent candle flames from blowing out in sudden drafts. Tall and curvy, the hurricane glass is a prime pick for tiki drinks and other tropical favorites, with its fluted rim providing ample room for flowers and festive garnishes.

Garnishes + Embellishments

Garnishes deserve far more attention than being an afterthought or treated as "just" the finishing touch to a drink.

For starters, our choice of garnish influences the aesthetics of the drink. Garnishes can range from straightforward and practical to elaborate, innovative creations that add a theatrical element, infusing a sense of excitement and anticipation.

The well-chosen garnish isn't simply for show—it brings substance to the drink. Seemingly small touches add subtle aromatics and flavors, enhancing the cocktail experience.

Selecting the best garnish for a drink is an art form and something to consider throughout the process of developing your drink. We want the garnish to make sense, whether it's a reflection of the ingredients or offering elements that otherwise complement the drink.

Most garnishes are derived from or relate to the liquid ingredients. A lemon wedge, wheel, twist, or swath (peel), for example, is an easy fit for a cocktail containing lemon juice; strawberry slices work well as garnish for drinks made with muddled strawberries. Exceptions to this rule include tiki-style drinks, sangrias, and the Bloody Mary—embellishments for these types of drinks can be an anything-and-everything-kitchen-sink style of thing, where more is more and bigger is almost always-better.

The citrus peel is the go-to of cocktail garnishes. While there's nothing wrong with garnishing simply with a wedge or wheel of citrus, taking the extra step to express the oils from the peel will enhance and balance the drink's flavors and sweetness.

Start by peeling back a thin layer of citrus peel, preferably with a Y peeler, though a vegetable peeler will do. To express the oils, hold the strip of citrus peel horizontally, with the outside of the skin facing away from you. Using both hands, with fingers along the top edge and thumbs along the bottom, carefully pinch the top and bottom to crease the peel lengthwise, releasing a fine mist of citrus oils from the outer skin.

Non-citrus fruit embellishments are also popular—and incredibly easy. They may dress a drink as wedges, slices, wheels, and half-wheels. Berries, cherries, cucumber ribbons, and melon balls are an effortless finish to any drink. Or get creative with small cookie cutters or a paring knife to cut larger fruits (think pineapple or watermelon) into fun shapes for a simple yet effective way to immediately elevate your garnish game.

Herbs are another category of garnish to consider, and one of our favorites. Fresh additions such as rosemary, thyme, lavender, mint, basil, and shiso add a powerful dimension to your creations both visually and aromatically.

Select an herb that either complements the flavors of the drink or was used as an ingredient. Fresh herbs, for example, can be muddled, infused to make an Eat Fit simple syrup, or incorporated with a light shake along with the liquid ingredients to strike a perfect flavor balance. (If you do opt for the shake to infuse directly into your drink, we recommend double straining—nobody wants a rogue rosemary quill in their teeth!)

Torching herbs, like rosemary, is another innovative way to manipulate the garnish itself. The goal is not to actually *burn* the herb but instead to lightly toast it, bringing out the herb's essential oils to create a smoky herbaceousness.

Speaking of, fire itself can serve as a garnish—an incredibly eye-catching one, at that. Flaming beverages typically need a high-proof alcohol for ignition, so we don't cover any in this book. We also recommend leaving the flames to the professionals.

Flowers are a simple, elegant way to add beauty to any drink. Use caution, though, as many flowers aren't edible and in fact, some can be quite dangerous. Conveniently, many grocery stores offer prepackaged food-safe flowers (look in the produce section). Farmers markets are also a good source for edible flowers. If you're pulling from your own backyard, stick with the familiar: lavender, pansies, orchids, roses, and violas.

As for other edible garnishes, the sky—or really, our level of creativity—is the limit. We love drinks finished with dark chocolate shavings, pickled vegetables, stuffed olives, or ginger candied with Swerve. Our editor Melanie has even used *venison* as a garnish—proving that there truly is no right or wrong.

Have fun with it, exploring inedible embellishments. There are paper umbrellas, of course, or jazz it up with Mardi Gras beads, feathers, figurines, playing cards, origami, flags, swizzle sticks, even candles or sparklers (carefully, of course). If you like it, roll with it!

Rimming glassware with salt (think sea salt, pink Himalayan salt, or black lava salt), Creole or jerk seasoning blends, or a sweetener like Swerve adds an extra touch both visually and in terms of complexity. Dipping the rim in lemon juice, lime juice, or Eat Fit Simple Syrup adds flavor and helps to ensure that the powdery garnishes stick to the rim of the glass. We often prefer to rim just half of the glass, to give people the option of sipping with or without.

Whatever garnish or embellishment you choose, be mindful of how it relates to the ingredients and the expression of the cocktail. Don't be afraid to get creative with ingredients—the simplest edits in terms of how they are sliced, folded, skewered, or even affixed to the glassware can dramatically change the cocktail experience.

Zero Proof Picks

The zero proof spirits category is expanding at a stunningly rapid pace, with an alcohol-free alternative for virtually every type of cocktail ingredient. This steady rise is a reflection of the shift in culture, with more people choosing to dial back or eliminate their consumption of alcohol, whatever the reason may be. If products that mimic alcoholic beverages are a trigger for you, it's best to avoid these items.

As always, we want to be sure that expectations are well managed. Though many brands have done an incredible job at replicating the characteristics of full-proof spirits, we find that many alcohol-free versions have just a whisper of something "missing," whether it be body, flavor, or bite. Entering into the zero proof culture with a sense of open-mindedness, fun, adventure, and experimentation is key.

The array of zero proof spirits, wine, and beer can feel a bit overwhelming, so we've assembled a list of our favorite booze-free items to add to the mix of your home bar. We also know that, by the time you're holding this book, many more products will have hit the market, and this list may look completely different. For now, however, here's a rundown of our go-to zero proof spirits, wine, and beer.

Spirits

Best Overall: Seedlip

Per ounce: 0 calories, 0 carbohydrate, 0 sugar

Seedlip doesn't brand its spirits as gin alternatives, though the botanical aromatics are most reminiscent of this spirit. Each of the three Seedlip varieties (Spice 94, Garden 108, and Grove 42) offers unique application and mixability, whether it be in your own craft masterpiece or simply by adding our Eat Fit Ginger Simple Syrup and sparkling water. In 2019, liquor and beer powerhouse DIAGEO acquired majority share of Seedlip, which is especially cool as it increases access, supplying the brand to over 25 countries.

Best Whiskey: Spiritless Kentucky 74 + Ritual Zero Proof Whiskey Alternative

Per ounce: 7.5 calories, 2 grams carbohydrate, less than 1 gram sugar

Designed specifically for cocktails, Kentucky 74 provides everything you want and expect from your favorite Bluegrass spirit: caramel, vanilla, oak. It made our list of favorites because it not only mixes like whiskey but also can also be enjoyed on the rocks or with bitters for that smooth finish.

Pro tip: Ritual Zero Proof Whiskey Alternative has more of that burn that brown-liquor aficionados have come to expect. To replicate this, we recommend going half and half with Kentucky 74 and Ritual, for a solid mix of flavor and bite. The creators of Kentucky 74 crafted it with a no- and low-model in mind, often recommending mixing their product with full-proof bourbon for a lower-ABV option, so we hope they will approve of our suggestion.

Best White Rum: Lyre's White Cane

Per ounce: 4.5 calories, 1 gram carbohydrate, less than 1 gram sugar

Vying with Kentucky 74 for most versatile spirit, this rum alternative works well across the board with a variety of drink styles, particularly tropical cocktails. Sweet aromas of alcohol on the nose along with oak, orange, and coconut on the palate might fool you into thinking this is the full-proof spirit.

Best Gin: Ritual Zero Proof Gin Alternative

Per ounce: 0 calories, 1 gram carbohydrate, less than 1 gram sugar

If you like your martini classic with a lemon twist, Ritual Zero Proof Gin Alternative has the high botanical fragrances and flavor profile and that satisfying burn you likely seek. Don't: use it for a dirty martini. It gets weird—and not in a good way. Olive juice does not combine well with the natural botanicals in this product. Do: opt for stirred over shaken to preserve the nose, taste, and spice.

Best Tequila: Ritual Zero Proof Tequila Alternative

Per ounce: 0 calories, less than 1 gram carbohydrate, less than 1 gram sugar

This products works best when mixed into a fresh-lime margarita with an orange slice and thyme (one of our favorite combinations). Ritual Zero Proof Tequila Alternative provides the earthy flavors of vanilla spice, guava, lime, and of course, blue agave that we typically expect from the full-proof spirit. There also is an element of smoke that mezcal fans will appreciate.

Best Liqueur: Lyre's Zero Proof Orange Sec

Per ounce: 20 calories, 5 grams carbohydrate, 5 grams sugar

A solid supplementary ingredient in many a zero proof cocktail, Lyre's Zero Proof Orange Sec brings the sweetness of Triple Sec without the heavy load of sugar. Its soft sweetness is pleasantly complemented by orange peel and rhubarb. Go easy, though; a little can go a long way.

We would be remiss to have a book full of delicious zero proof cocktail recipes and not touch on some of the ready-to-drink products already available on the market: nonalcoholic wine and beer!

Wine

Best Sparkling Wine: Thomson & Scott Noughty | Chardonnay Sparkling
Per 4 ounces: 17.5 calories, 3.6 grams carbohydrate, 3.6 grams sugar
This certified organic sparkling Chardonnay crafted from the sandy terroir of southern Spain is the real deal. Even the most ardent champagne lovers will be fooled by Noughty's crisp apple notes, elegant pale coloring, and persistent effervescence. It is decadent on its own but versatile enough to work with a variety of zero proof cocktails. You'll want a bottle on hand for all of your celebrations to offer an alternative to anyone not drinking for any reason.

Best Red Wine: Sovi | Red Blend

Per 8-ounce can: 20 calories, 1 gram carbohydrate, 1 gram sugar
This dealcoholized red is partially oak aged with notes of black raspberry, dark cherry, and baking spices. We think Sovi Red Blend, with its well-rounded acidity and exquisitely dry finish, is a nice alternative for Pinot Noir and Cabernet lovers alike.

Best White Wine: Waterbrook | Clean Chardonnay

Per 4 ounces: 10 calories, 2 grams carbohydrate, 1 gram sugar
Waterbrook, a Washington-based winery with expert winemakers at the helm, creates a dealcoholized masterpiece that brings notes of both peaches and Golden Delicious apples while still representing the oak, honey, and vanilla expected of American Chardonnay.

Beer

Best Lager: Heineken 0.0

Per 11.2 ounces: 69 calories, 16 grams carbohydrate, 4.3 grams sugar
Slightly thinner than the Dutch favorite, this nonalcoholic version maintains the characteristic sharp flavor and lip-puckering effect that fans of the original know and love, balanced with refreshingly fruity notes and a softer, malty body. Getting down to brass tacks, Heineken 0.0 is your

average easy-drinking lager that's also readily available at local retailers, restaurants, bars, and sports venues.

Best IPA: Surreal Brewing Company | Juicy Mavs

Per 12 ounces: 25 calories, 4.9 grams carbohydrate, 0 sugar

This Hazy IPA maintains the classic taste, feel, and aroma of a hoppy, hazy beer. Full bodied with characteristic IPA foam, Juicy Mavs is delightfully crisp and balanced with a subtle, clean malt finish.

Best Amber: Athletic Brewing Co. | Cerveza Atletica

Per 12 ounces: 60 calories, 15 grams carbohydrate, 3 grams sugar

With its rich caramel color and slightest tinge of hops, Athletic Brewing's Cerveza Atletica drinks more like an Amber lager. The flavor has a moderate sweetness comparable to New Belgium Brewing's Fat Tire, but overall this easy sipper is mellow and light enough for a hot day.

Best Stout: Surreal Brewing Company | 17 Mile Porter

Per 12 ounces: 50 calories, 10.5 grams carbohydrate, 0 sugar

17 Mile Porter is a full-on porter with strong chocolate, campfire notes on the nose. The chocolate becomes quite bitter on the palate, expressing roasted espresso and a silky, medium finish. We can imagine this as a solid replacement for Murphy's Irish Stout or to replace a stout in your favorite recipes.

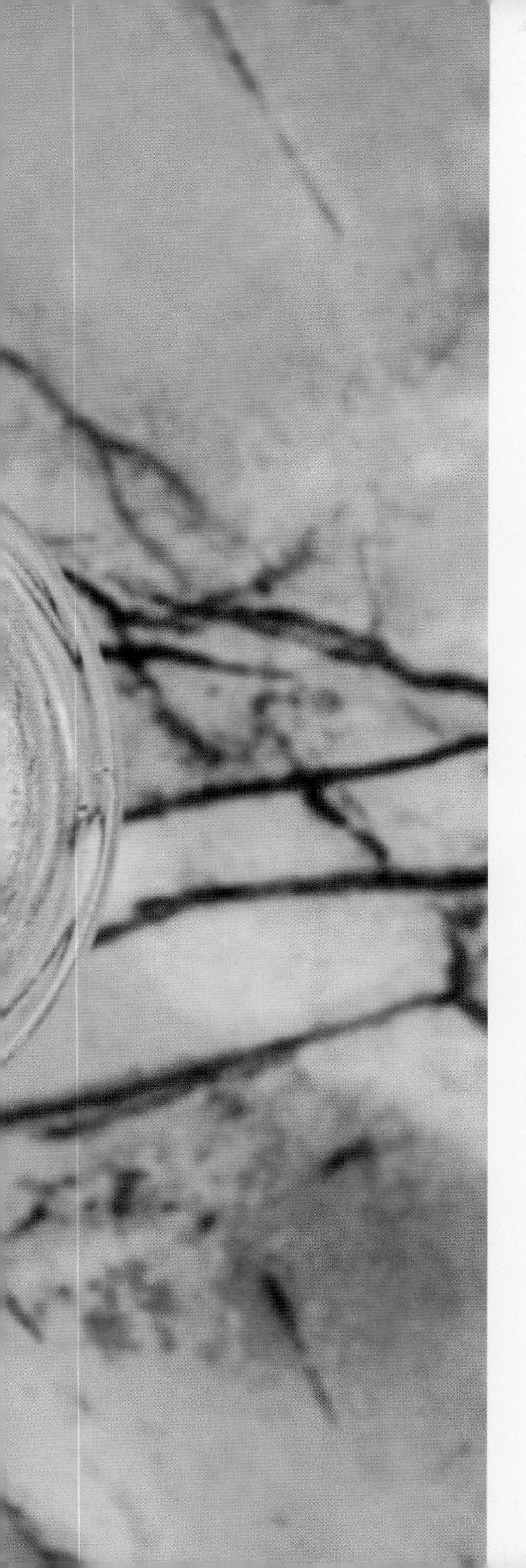

New Orleans + Classics

These unforgettable cocktails transcend time, inspiring modern masterpieces and craft creations alike. One thing is certain—they will never go out of style.

A word to the wise: the drinks that follow are classics reworked to work within the Eat Fit nutritional guidelines—namely, dialing back the sugar—and to of course also be zero proof. We share this to say it's important to take your first sip with an open mind, expecting a fresh spin on traditional favorites.

Old Fashioned

The Eat Fit Collection

Makes 1 serving

Bitters are traditionally added directly over a sugar cube to make an Old Fashioned, with no muddling of the orange or cherry. In this zero proof version, however, Ethan opted for the muddle and skipped the sweetener, since the orange, cherry, and zero proof whiskey offer a natural sweetness.

INGREDIENTS

¼ orange, suprêmed

1 pitted cherry

4 dashes Angostura bitters

2 ounces zero proof whiskey

1 large ice sphere or cube

Orange half-wheel and peel, for garnish

Cherry, for garnish

Bamboo pick

METHOD

In a rocks glass, gently press the orange and cherry. Add Angostura bitters and zero proof whiskey, then add ice and stir. Garnish with a combination of orange half-wheel, orange peel, and cherry on bamboo pick.

NUTRITION

45 calories, 0 fat, 0 saturated fat, 0 sodium, 9 grams net carbs, 0 fiber, 5 grams sugar (1 gram added sugar), 0 protein

GF, Vegan, Low Carb

Suprême /

Pronounced "su-prem," it's a French technique that sounds fancy, but it's just the process of removing the membrane from citrus segments.

Pro Tip /

When it comes to ice for this drink, bigger is better. Larger cubes minimize the surface area exposed so as to not dilute the drink.

Manhattan

The Eat Fit Collection

Makes 1 serving

Pleasantly tart and mildly sweet, hibiscus tea brings a fresh twist to this multidimensional cocktail.

INGREDIENTS

1½ ounces zero proof whiskey

1 ounce brewed hibiscus tea, chilled

1 tablespoon Eat Fit Simple Syrup (*recipe on page 39*)

2 dashes Angostura bitters

Ice

1 dark cherry, stem removed

METHOD

Combine zero proof whiskey, hibiscus tea, Eat Fit Simple Syrup, and Angostura bitters in a Yarai glass. Add ice and stir. Strain into a glass and add cherry.

NUTRITION

20 calories, 0 fat, 0 saturated fat, 0 sodium, 4 grams net carbs, 0 fiber, 2 grams sugar (1 gram added sugar), 0 protein

GF, Vegan, Low Carb

Playing Favorites /

We're open to a variety of brands when it comes to zero proof spirits. But when a bourbon or whiskey replacer is needed, we feel strongly that a blend of Ritual Whiskey with Spiritless Kentucky 74 is best.

Sazerac

The Eat Fit Collection

Makes 1 serving

Zero proof or otherwise, the Sazerac is timeless. Traditional recipes call for a sugar cube muddled with bitters; we opted to forgo a sugar replacer since the zero proof whiskey brings a natural sweetness to the drink. If you've mastered your own specific way to make a Sazerac, then simply let these ingredients inspire you to make it your own.

INGREDIENTS

2 ounces zero proof whiskey

4 dashes Peychaud's bitters

1 dash Angostura bitters

Ice

Lemon twist, for garnish

METHOD

Combine all liquid ingredients in a Yarai glass. Add ice and stir. Strain into a rocks glass and garnish with lemon twist.

NUTRITION

35 calories, 0 fat, 0 saturated fat, 0 sodium, 6 grams net carbs, 0 fiber, 1 gram sugar (1 gram added sugar), 0 protein

GF, Vegan, Low Carb

History Lesson /

In 2008, the Crescent City became the first American city to have an official cocktail when the Louisiana House of Representatives voted to proclaim the Sazerac the cocktail of New Orleans.

Posmo

The Eat Fit Collection

Makes 1 serving

Our Posmo is a riff on the modern classic Cosmo, only it is made with pomegranate in place of cranberry juice. Unlike the Cosmopolitan, however, this variation should only be called a Posmo. Try saying Posmopolitan out loud a time or two, and you'll probably agree.

INGREDIENTS

1½ ounces zero proof vodka

1 tablespoon Lyre's Zero Proof Orange Sec

1 tablespoon pomegranate juice

½ tablespoon lime juice

Ice

Lime wheel, for garnish

METHOD

Combine all liquid ingredients in a shaker tin with ice and shake vigorously. Double strain into a martini glass and garnish with lime wheel.

NUTRITION

20 calories, 0 fat, 0 saturated fat, 0 sodium, 5 grams net carbs, 0 fiber, 5 grams sugar (2 grams added sugar), 0 protein

GF, Vegan, Low Carb

Juice /

Pomegranate, dark cherry, or 100 percent cranberry juice can be used interchangeably. They're all antioxidant rich—but they're also all high in natural sugars, which is why we use just a smidge.

French 75

The Eat Fit Collection

Makes 1 serving

The French 75 was named after the French 75-millimeter field gun celebrated for its rapid-fire power. The original, made with cognac—and even its lighter gin-based sister—is a wickedly powerful concoction. This zero proof version maintains the respect of the original's potency without knocking you out.

INGREDIENTS

1 ounce zero proof gin

2 tablespoons lemon juice

1 tablespoon Eat Fit Simple Syrup (*recipe on page 39*)

Ice

4 ounces zero proof sparkling wine

Lemon swath, expressed, for garnish

METHOD

Combine gin, lemon juice, and Eat Fit Simple Syrup in a small shaker tin filled with ice. Shake and double strain into a tall champagne flute. Top with zero proof sparkling wine and garnish with expressed lemon swath.

NUTRITION

25 calories, 0 fat, 0 saturated fat, 0 sodium, 6 grams net carbs, 0 fiber, 4 grams sugar (0 added sugar), 0 protein

GF, Vegan, Low Carb

Pro Tip /

The lemon juice really fizzes up the sparkling wine. Tilt the champagne flute as you pour the sparkling wine to keep it from overflowing.

Espresso Martini

The Eat Fit Collection

Makes 1 serving

Sweet and creamy, you'd never guess this decadent, velvety drink is also completely plant based.

INGREDIENTS

1 tablespoon Swerve granular

1½ ounces brewed hot espresso

1½ ounces zero proof vodka

½ teaspoon pure vanilla extract

1 tablespoon canned coconut milk, full fat, unsweetened

Ice

METHOD

Add Swerve to hot espresso and stir to dissolve. Combine espresso mixture with remaining liquid ingredients in a shaker tin. Add ice, shake vigorously, and double strain into a martini glass or novelty glass of choice.

NUTRITION

40 calories, 3 grams fat, 2.5 grams saturated fat, 10 mg sodium, 1 gram net carbs, 0 fiber, 0 sugar, 0 protein

GF, Vegan, Low Carb

Tip /

Look for quality canned coconut milk that is unsweetened, with a simple ingredient list of just coconut and water.

Espresso /

Whatever works best for you works for this drink. It can be a freshly brewed shot of espresso or 1 or 2 teaspoons instant espresso powder dissolved in hot water.

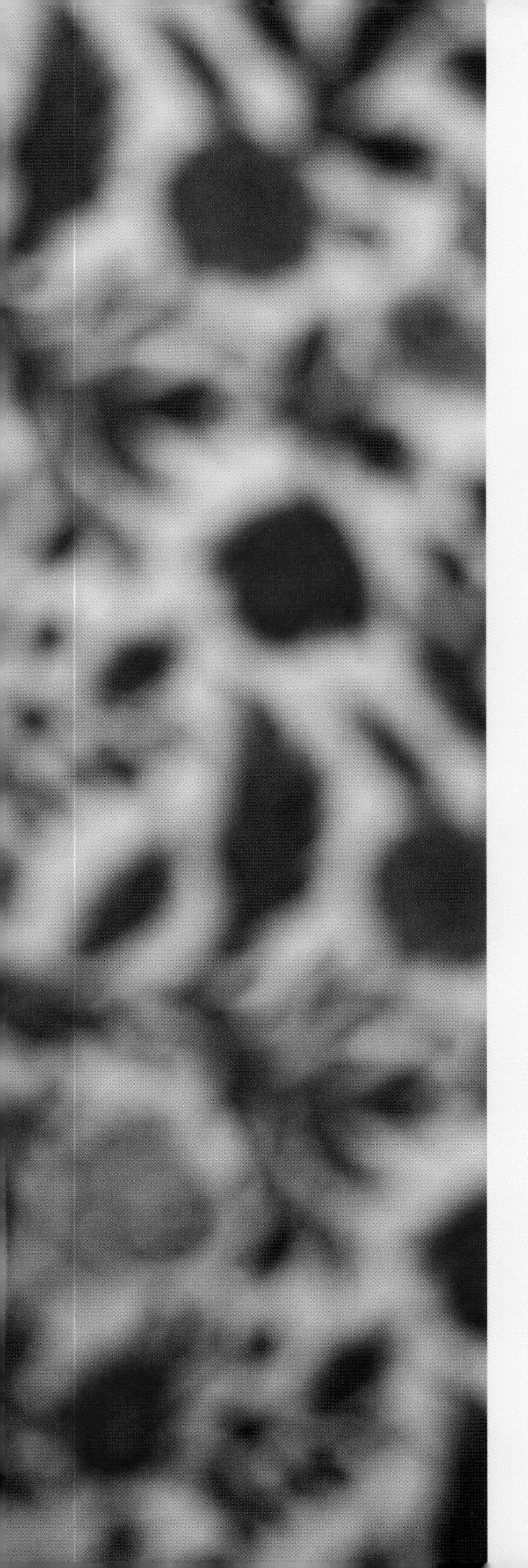

Herbal + Florals

Aromatics are integral elements of a cocktail, influencing our perception from the first scent through the last drop. Rosemary, rose, and mint are just a few of the herbal and floral essences you'll find layered into these zero proof drinks, fresh and inviting with every sip.

The Amelia

Inspired by The Eli | Monroe

Makes 1 serving

The contrast of black lava salt with the vividly hued blend of Seedlip and blackberries gives The Amelia a wow factor that belies the simplicity of this recipe.

INGREDIENTS

3 tablespoons Rosemary Simple Syrup (*recipe on page 39*)

Lava (black) rock salt, finely crushed

5 blackberries (reserve 1 for garnish)

1 tablespoon Lyre's Zero Proof Orange Sec

2 ounces Seedlip Grove 42 Citrus

1 tablespoon lemon juice

1 tablespoon spring water

Ice

Mint (or basil) leaf, for garnish

Bamboo pick

METHOD

Rim half of a coupe or novelty glass with a touch of Rosemary Simple Syrup, then dip into lava rock salt. Shake off any excess before filling the glass.

Muddle blackberries in a shaker tin, then add remaining Rosemary Simple Syrup, orange sec, Seedlip, lemon juice, water, and ice. Shake vigorously and double strain into glass.

Garnish with the single remaining blackberry wrapped with a mint leaf, secured with bamboo pick.

NUTRITION

30 calories, 0 fat, 0 saturated fat, 95 mg sodium, 5 grams net carbs, 2 grams fiber, 5 grams sugar (2 grams added sugar), 0 protein

GF, Vegan, Low Carb

Lava Salt /

Activated charcoal gives lava salt its deep black color. Use a mortar and pestle or small food processor to finely grind the salt into a sand-like grain to best rim the glass. If you can't get your hands on black salt, finely crushed sea salt will provide a similar flavor, just without the dramatic contrast.

Rosarito

Inspired by Don Juanz Baja Beach Tacos | Shreveport

Makes 1 serving

Crisp and fresh, each drink delivers a dose of 100 milligrams of turmeric, a natural anti-inflammatory compound that supports our whole-body wellness.

INGREDIENTS

2 tablespoons blood orange juice

1 tablespoon lime juice

3 mint leaves

1 tablespoon Eat Fit Simple Syrup (*recipe on page 39*)

½ teaspoon turmeric

1 large ice cube

Sparkling mineral water, to top

Orange peel, for garnish

Lighter

Bamboo pick

METHOD

Combine orange juice, lime juice, mint leaves, and Eat Fit Simple Syrup in a Yarai glass. Add turmeric and stir or whisk with a fork to dissolve. Strain into a rocks glass over ice cube, top with mineral water, and give a light stir.

Garnish with a flamed orange peel curled over rim or around bamboo pick.

NUTRITION

20 calories, 0 fat, 0 saturated fat, 0 sodium, 5 grams net carbs, 0 fiber, 3 grams sugar (0 added sugar), 0 protein

GF, Vegan, Low Carb

Tip /

Rose petals have been used to infuse preserves and syrups for centuries. Be sure to use edible or culinary-grade dried rose petals, typically found at specialty tea stores (and online, of course).

A Little R&R

Inspired by Commander's Palace | NOLA

Makes 1 serving

We can always count on Commander's Palace in New Orleans to elevate the ordinary, upgrading this simple spritzer with rose-infused syrup and dashes of bitters. It turns out that this drink came about by accident: Commander's Palace somehow ended up with dried rosebuds instead of lavender for one of its specialty drinks. They played around with it to create a rose simple syrup that would become the inspiration for A Little R&R.

INGREDIENTS

1 strawberry, sliced (reserve 1 slice for garnish)

Ice

3 ounces sparkling water

1½ tablespoons lemon juice

1½ tablespoons Rose Simple Syrup (*recipe below*)

3-4 dashes rhubarb bitters

Bamboo pick

METHOD

Add strawberry slices to a small wine glass, followed by 4 cubes of ice and sparkling water. Combine lemon juice, Rose Simple Syrup, and bitters in a small shaker tin with additional ice. Shake vigorously and strain into the glass. Garnish with strawberry slice on bamboo pick.

ROSE SIMPLE SYRUP

¼ cup dehydrated rose petals

8 ounces Swoon simple syrup

METHOD

Combine ingredients and let infuse at room temperature for 24 to 48 hours. Strain and refrigerate unused syrup for up to 4 weeks.

NUTRITION

10 calories, 0 fat, 0 saturated fat, 10 mg sodium, 2 grams net carbs, 0 fiber, 1 gram sugar (0 added sugar), 0 protein

GF, Vegan, Low Carb

Add a Muddle /

For deeper strawberry flavor and color, muddle 1 or 2 extra strawberries in the bottom of the glass before building this drink.

The Rosemary 94

Inspired by Restaurant Cotton | Monroe

Makes 1 serving

Lovely and light, this wonderfully balanced drink just makes us feel like we're sipping something special.

INGREDIENTS

2 ounces Seedlip Spice 94 Aromatic

3 tablespoons Rosemary Simple Syrup (*recipe on page 39*)

2 teaspoons lime juice

2 teaspoons lemon juice

Ice

Rosemary sprig, for garnish

Kitchen torch or lighter

METHOD

Combine all liquid ingredients in a small shaker tin filled with ice. Double strain into a chilled novelty glass and garnish with torched rosemary.

NUTRITION

5 calories, 0 fat, 0 saturated fat, 0 sodium, 2 grams net carbs, 0 fiber, 0 sugar, 0 protein

GF, Vegan, Low Carb

Torching Tip /

Using a kitchen torch or lighter, flame the rosemary just until it begins to smoke. The idea is to bring out the herb's essential oils, creating a smoky herbaceousness that infuses the drink (not to scorch it to a crisp).

Sweet + Spicy

Nothing says Louisiana like a little sweet heat. Striking a balance in that delicate space between sweet and spice, these cocktails bring the flavor without overpowering your palate.

Quest Like A Tribe Does

Inspired by City Pork Brasserie & Bar | Baton Rouge

Makes 1 serving

This wonderfully savory drink is a delightfully unexpected blend of coconut milk with lemongrass, ginger, and chili oil. If you close your eyes and take a sip, you just might think you're enjoying a street drink in Thailand. (While we try not to play favorites, this just might be Molly, Ethan, and Melanie's favorite cocktail in the book.)

INGREDIENTS

2 tablespoons canned coconut milk, full fat, unsweetened

½ ounce Seedlip Garden 108 Herbal

½ tablespoon lime juice

½ tablespoon grated gingerroot (approximately half a knob of ginger)

½ tablespoon Lemongrass Simple Syrup (*recipe below*)

Ice

3-5 drops chili oil or tincture

Lime zest, for garnish

Edible flower, for garnish

METHOD

Shake can of coconut milk well to mix solids and liquids. Combine coconut milk, Seedlip, lime juice, ginger, and Lemongrass Simple Syrup in a small shaker tin with ice. Shake and double strain into a chilled martini glass. Top with 3-5 drops of chili oil. Garnish with lime zest and an edible flower.

LEMONGRASS SIMPLE SYRUP

1 cup water

½ cup Swerve granular or 1½ cups granular allulose

2 stalks lemongrass

METHOD

In a small saucepan, bring water to a boil. Reduce to medium-high heat and add sweetener. Stir to dissolve and continue to heat for 10 minutes. Trim lemongrass stalks into 3-inch pieces and add to mixture. Transfer to heat-safe glass container and allow to infuse for at least 1 hour. Double strain before using. Refrigerate unused portion in a sealed airtight container for up to 4 weeks.

NUTRITION

60 calories, 6 grams fat, 4 grams saturated fat, 5 mg sodium, 2 grams net carbs, 0 fiber, 0 sugar, 0 protein

GF, Vegan, Low Carb

Decorative Drops /

A medicine-style dropper provides precision and control for placing the drops of chili oil just so. If you don't have a dropper, dip a cocktail straw into the chili oil, placing your thumb on the top of the straw to hold the oil until you release it onto the drink. It's less precise than a dropper but will still do the trick.

Broadmoor Norteño

Inspired by Zuzul Coastal Cuisine | Shreveport

Makes 1 serving

This drink is a riff on a riff on the Matador, a popular tequila-based drink. The original Matador Norteño is made with another agave-based spirit called sotol. Chef Gabriel puts his mark on this Broadmoor Norteño with his house-made habanero tincture and pineapple syrup, which we carried over into the Eat Fit version, featuring zero proof tequila.

INGREDIENTS

1½ ounces zero proof tequila

3 tablespoons Pineapple Simple Syrup (*recipe below*)

3 drops Habanero Tincture (*recipe below*) or 1 habanero seed

1 tablespoon lemon juice

Ice

Edible flower, for garnish

METHOD

Combine all liquid ingredients in small shaker tin with ice. Double strain into a novelty glass and garnish with a floating edible flower.

PINEAPPLE SIMPLE SYRUP

1 cup water

½ cup Swerve granular or 1½ cups granular allulose

2 cups pureed pineapple

METHOD

In a medium saucepan, bring water to a boil. Reduce to medium-high heat and add sweetener. Stir to dissolve and continue to heat for 10 minutes. Fold in pineapple puree. Remove from heat and allow to steep for 10 minutes. Double strain into a heat-safe container before using. Refrigerate unused portion in a sealed airtight container for up to 4 weeks.

HABANERO TINCTURE

2 large habanero chile peppers

6 ounces spring water

METHOD

Remove the stems from peppers, and slice peppers into rings. Place pepper rings (including seeds) in a jar and add water. Tighten lid and allow mixture to infuse no less than 4 hours. Keep in mind, these habaneros are crazy hot. Consider wearing disposable gloves, don't touch your face, and be sure to wash your hands thoroughly after handling.

NUTRITION

20 calories, 0 fat, 0 saturated fat, 20 mg sodium, 6 grams net carbs, 0 fiber, 3 grams sugar (0 added sugar), 0 protein

GF, Vegan, Low Carb

The Blueberry Fall

Inspired by Pyre Provisions | Northshore

Makes 1 serving

> Blueberry Basil Spritz was the original name for this drink. Then Hope—our Eat Fit Monroe dietitian and photographer for this book—took a tumble from atop a chair while trying to get the perfect overhead shot. That's how The Blueberry Fall was born.

INGREDIENTS

2½ ounces Blueberry Simple Syrup (*recipe below*)

Ice

4 ounces sparkling water

Fresh basil, for garnish

Habanero ring, for garnish

METHOD

Pour Blueberry Simple Syrup into rocks glass. Add ice and top with sparkling water. Gently stir and garnish with fresh basil and habanero ring.

BLUEBERRY SIMPLE SYRUP

Makes approximately 2½ cups

1 cup water

½ cup Swerve granular or 1½ cups granular allulose

2 cups blueberries

2 habanero chile peppers, seeded (optional)

METHOD

In a medium saucepan, bring water to a boil. Reduce to medium-high heat and add sweetener. Stir to dissolve and continue to heat for 10 minutes. In a food processor, blend blueberries and seeded habanero chile peppers until smooth. Fold blueberry-habanero mixture into simple syrup. Allow to steep for 10 minutes. Pour into a heat-safe container before using. Refrigerate unused portion for up to 1 week.

NUTRITION

25 calories, 0 fat, 0 saturated fat, 15 mg sodium, 5 grams net carbs, 1 gram fiber, 4 grams sugar (0 added sugar), 0 protein

GF, Vegan, Low Carb

El Espíritu Rita

Inspired by Tchoup's MidCity Smokehouse | Acadiana

Makes 1 serving

This smoky 'rita designed by bar manager Nathan Walker has everything we want in a margarita and then some. The heat, the sweet, the *drama*—every note builds interest and keeps us coming back for more.

INGREDIENTS

1 lime wedge, to rim glass

Sea salt, to rim glass

2 ounces zero proof tequila

2 tablespoons Oleo Saccharum (*recipe on page 41*)

½ tablespoon Swoon simple syrup

1 tablespoon lime juice

2 slices fresh jalapeño (reserve 1 slice for garnish)

Ice (preferably 1 large cube)

Lime half-wheel (grilled or torched), for garnish

Bamboo pick

METHOD

Run the lime wedge along half the rim of your glass of choice, then dip that rim into salt. Shake off any excess before filling the glass.

Combine all liquid ingredients and 1 slice jalapeño in a small shaker tin with ice. Shake and double strain over ice cube into glass.

Garnish with 1 jalapeño slice and grilled lime half-wheel layered on bamboo pick.

NUTRITION

10 calories, 0 fat, 0 saturated fat, 170 mg sodium, 4 grams net carbs, 0 fiber, 1 gram sugar (0 added sugar), 0 protein

GF, Vegan, Low Carb

Fun Fact /

Bar manager Nathan Walker is also a fashion designer; two of his gowns have been showcased on the red carpet at the Emmy Awards.

Ball

Rebellion

Inspired by Mestizo Louisiana Mexican Cuisine | Baton Rouge

Makes 1 serving

Mestizo chef-owner Jim Urdiales has so many zero-sugar drinks on the menu that the bigger challenge was selecting which one to feature. We opted for this multifaceted cocktail, drawn to its striking layers of heat, sweet, and citrus.

INGREDIENTS

1½ ounces zero proof tequila

2 tablespoons lime juice

2 tablespoons Eat Fit Simple Syrup (*recipe on page 39*)

1½ ounces passionfruit tea, chilled

1 thin slice fresh jalapeño

1 orange slice

4 thin slices cucumber

Sparkling water, to top

Ice

Edible flower or cucumber slice, for garnish

METHOD

Add the first 7 ingredients to a shaker tin. Shake vigorously and strain into glass of your choice. Top with sparkling water, then ice. Give a light stir and garnish with choice of edible flower or cucumber slice.

NUTRITION

10 calories, 0 fat, 0 saturated fat, 20 mg sodium, 4 grams net carbs, 0 fiber, 0 sugar, 0 protein

GF, Vegan, Low Carb

Mango Scotch Bonnet

Inspired by Taylor'd Eatz Caribbean Food Truck | Shreveport

Makes 1 serving

Mangos add a touch of sweetness while the scotch bonnet brings that unmistakable Jamaican heat, as if you are sipping the fresh, bold flavors of the Caribbean.

INGREDIENTS

1 scotch bonnet pepper

1 lime

Caribbean jerk seasoning, to rim glass

½ cup fresh mango

2 ounces zero proof rum

2 ounces spring water

1 tablespoon Lyre's Zero Proof Orange Sec

Ice

Bamboo pick

METHOD

Slice a scotch bonnet pepper into fourths. Save one fourth for garnish and chop one fourth. The remaining pepper will not be used in this recipe. Slice lime in half. Juice half and set aside. From the remaining half, slice 1 lime wheel for garnish and 1 lime wedge to rim the glass.

Run the lime wedge along rim of a rocks glass, then roll the rim in a shallow dish filled with jerk seasoning. Shake off any excess before filling the glass.

In a blender, add mango, lime juice, zero proof rum, water, orange sec, and chopped scotch bonnet pepper. Blend until smooth.

Add to a shaker tin filled with ice and shake. Double strain into rimmed glass and garnish with lime wheel and slice of scotch bonnet pepper threaded onto bamboo pick.

NUTRITION

80 calories, 0 fat, 0 saturated fat, 45 mg sodium, 19 grams net carbs, 2 grams fiber, 17 grams sugar (4 grams added sugar), 1 gram protein

GF, Vegan

Pro Tip /

While we always love fresh, frozen mangos also work perfectly for this drink.

Heat Advisory /

Don't let the mellow name of the scotch bonnet fool you; it is one feisty pepper. Reportedly as much as 80 times hotter than a jalapeño, the scotch pepper is to be handled with caution. Translation: wearing disposable gloves is not going overboard. Please don't touch your eyes or nose while you're handling these little guys.

Highballs + Collinses

Traditionally simple drinks made with no more than a few basic ingredients, this curated list of high-volume coolers enhances the conventional with twists such as ginger, pomegranate, dragon fruit, and orange blossom.

The Zydeco

Inspired by Buck & Johnny's | Acadiana

Makes 2 servings

This cocktail is like a cross between a strawberry daiquiri and a strawberry smoothie, in the most refreshing of ways.

INGREDIENTS

1 cup fresh or frozen strawberries, pureed

2 ounces Ginger Simple Syrup (*recipe on page 40*)

Ice

5 ounces sparkling water

Ginger peels, for garnish

Strawberry halves, for garnish

Bamboo picks

METHOD

Combine pureed strawberries and Ginger Simple Syrup in a small shaker tin. Shake and pour into glasses filled with ice. Add sparkling water to fill. Lightly stir and garnish with ginger peels and strawberry halves on bamboo picks.

NUTRITION

45 calories, 0 fat, 0 saturated fat, 10 mg sodium, 8 grams net carbs, 3 grams fiber, 7 grams sugar (0 added sugar), 1 gram protein

GF, Vegan, Low Carb

Haiku Zero

Inspired by Tsunami | NOLA

Makes 1 serving

Haiku Zero is not only a great name for a drink—it's also a fun play on words, representing what's inside: "hai" for hibiscus, "ku" for cucumber, and "zero," of course, because it's zero proof.

INGREDIENTS

2 cucumber slices, ¼ inch thick

2 ounces pomegranate juice

2 ounces brewed passionfruit tea, chilled

2 tablespoons Eat Fit Simple Syrup (*recipe on page 39*)

1 tablespoon lime juice

Ice

Pomegranate seeds, for garnish

Cucumber ribbon, for garnish

METHOD

Muddle cucumber in the bottom of a small shaker tin. Add pomegranate juice, passionfruit tea, Eat Fit Simple Syrup, and lime juice and shake. Double strain over ice in a Collins glass. Garnish with pomegranate seeds and cucumber ribbon.

NUTRITION

35 calories, 0 fat, 0 saturated fat, 5 mg sodium, 9 grams net carbs, 0 fiber, 8 grams sugar (0 added sugar), 0 protein

GF, Vegan, Low Carb

Pink Zombie

The Eat Fit Collection

Makes 1 serving

Electric pink with just the right amount of sparkly sweetness, this drink instantly ups the party vibe.

INGREDIENTS

2 tablespoons lime juice

1 tablespoon pineapple juice

1 tablespoon Eat Fit Simple Syrup (*recipe on page 39*)

1 ounce zero proof gin

4 dashes Angostura bitters

1 teaspoon dragon fruit powder

Ice

4 ounces sparkling water

3 raspberries, for garnish

METHOD

Combine lime juice, pineapple juice, Eat Fit Simple Syrup, zero proof gin, bitters, and dragon fruit powder in a shaker tin. Add ice and shake vigorously. In a hurricane glass, add sparkling water. Double strain contents of the shaker into glass and add ice. Garnish with raspberries or red fruit of choice.

NUTRITION

45 calories, 0 fat, 0 saturated fat, 10 mg sodium, 8 grams net carbs, 2 grams fiber, 5 grams sugar (0 added sugar), 1 gram protein

GF, Vegan, Low Carb

Dragon Fruit /

Also known as pitaya, dragon fruit has a mild flavor, often compared to kiwi and pear. Powdered dragon fruit has a deep pink-red color that immediately adds a magnificent hue to a variety of cocktails.

Heathrow Lounge

Inspired by SoBou | NOLA

Makes 1 serving

The inspiration for this cocktail came on a flight from Heathrow Airport in the UK to Louis Armstrong New Orleans International Airport. The idea was that passengers would fortify themselves with a hydrating, zero proof cocktail before landing in the full-proof spirit of the Big Easy.

INGREDIENTS

3 ounces brewed orange blossom tea, chilled

1 tablespoon lemon juice

2 tablespoons Eat Fit Simple Syrup (*recipe on page 39*)

2 drops New Orleans Orange Flower Water

Ice

Lemon wheel, for garnish

Mint sprig, for garnish

METHOD

Combine all liquid ingredients in a shaker tin. Add ice and shake. Double strain into a novelty glass of choice and garnish with lemon wheel and mint sprig.

NUTRITION

4 calories, 0 fat, 0 saturated fat, 0 sodium, 1 gram net carb, 0 fiber, 0 sugar, 0 protein

GF, Vegan, Low Carb

Orange Flower Water /

Traditionally used in aromatherapy, orange flower water is a highly potent tincture that is distilled from bitter orange blossoms. Find it at natural foods stores or Mediterranean markets, order online, or make it at home following our DIY guide for bitters.

Peach Mule

Inspired by Braiz'n American Bar & Grill | Monroe

Makes 1 serving

> Ginger beer tends to be high in sugar, so we opted for an Eat Fit Ginger Simple Syrup instead. While we adore this drink made with fresh peaches, feel free to mix it up to create an orange, blueberry, or strawberry mule.

INGREDIENTS

1 white or yellow peach, quartered

4 mint leaves

1 ounce Seedlip Grove 42 Citrus

1 tablespoon lime juice

1½ tablespoons Ginger Simple Syrup (*recipe on page 40*)

Ice

Sparkling water, to top

Peach slice, for garnish

Mint leaf, for garnish

Bamboo pick

METHOD

Muddle peach with mint leaves in a shaker tin. Add Seedlip, lime juice, Ginger Simple Syrup, and ice. Shake well.

Double strain into a Collins glass and top with ice and sparkling water.

Lightly stir and garnish with peach slice and mint leaf secured on bamboo pick.

NUTRITION

15 calories, 0 fat, 0 saturated fat, 5 mg sodium, 4 grams net carbs, 0 fiber, 3 grams sugar (0 added sugar), 0 protein

GF, Vegan, Low Carb

Waste Not, Want Not /

Save the strained, muddled peach-lime-ginger blend that's left behind to add to a smoothie, hot cereal, or even overnight oats.

Fizzes, Flips + Smashes

Ingredients such as egg white and fee foam bring a creamy feel and fun textural element to our fizz, flip, and smash. Fresh herbs and whole fruits shine center stage, lending aromatic notes and visual appeal.

Tip /

The glassware you pick is essential. This drink is delicious in any vessel, but to get the full visual impact of this multihued beauty, opt for a tall, slim glass like a Collins glass.

Hibiscus Fizz

Inspired by Café Vermilionville | Acadiana

Makes 1 serving

With striking layers of lavender and violet, building this drink is quite a show. The aerated egg-white layer fills the glass, then settles back as the deeper colors of the hibiscus tea move in. Together the ingredients create an alchemy that continues to evolve as we sip this silky drink.

INGREDIENTS

1 egg white

Ice

2 ounces brewed hibiscus tea, chilled

1½ tablespoons Eat Fit Simple Syrup (*recipe on page 39*)

2 ounces sparkling water

METHOD

Add egg white to a small shaker tin and shake vigorously for 1 minute. Fill the small half of the shaker tin with ice, assemble the shaker, and shake vigorously for an additional 45 seconds, aerating until it reaches a meringue-like consistency. (Even if you think you're shaking it intensely, kick it up a notch—this drink requires a little muscle. Think of it as a mini cardio session. The harder, faster, and longer you shake, the better!) The outside of the shaker will start to show heavy condensation and even little ice crystals.

Add hibiscus tea and Eat Fit Simple Syrup and shake for another 30 seconds. In a Collins glass, add sparkling water. Strain contents of the shaker over sparkling water. Give it a minute; the liquid will start to pour at a slower rate. As the egg white foam starts to come though, slide the strainer top back just a bit to allow the foam to continue to pour without plopping.

NUTRITION

15 calories, 0 fat, 0 saturated fat, 65 mg sodium, 0 net carb, 0 fiber, 0 sugar, 4 grams protein

GF, Low Carb

Make It Vegan /

Trade out the egg white for 2 tablespoons aquafaba, the liquid drained from canned chickpeas. Wild as it may seem, this chickpea juice is really a magical little egg-white replacer that whips and creates a meringue-like foam.

The Picard Flip

Inspired by Commander's Palace | NOLA

Makes 1 serving

The Commander's Palace team whipped up this silky, creamy concoction just for us. The "flip" is an old-school style of cocktail with core ingredients traditionally including some type of spirit along with egg white, sugar, and spice. In this case, the tea substitutes for the spirit and imparts the spice component. As for the name, bartender David Wheelahan is a tremendous "Star Trek" fan—and Earl Grey is Captain Picard's drink of choice.

INGREDIENTS

1 egg white

5 ice cubes

2 ounces brewed Earl Grey tea, chilled

1 tablespoon orange juice

1 tablespoon lime juice

1 tablespoon Swoon simple syrup

½ teaspoon pure vanilla extract

2 tablespoons sparkling water

Lime wheel, for garnish

METHOD

Add egg white to a small shaker tin and shake vigorously for 1 minute. Add ice and shake for an additional minute, aerating until it reaches a meringue-like consistency. Add Earl Grey tea, orange juice, and lime juice and shake for another 30 seconds. Add Swoon simple syrup and vanilla and give it one more light shake. In a coupe glass, add sparkling water. Double strain contents of the shaker over sparkling water and garnish with lime wheel.

NUTRITION

35 calories, 0 fat, 0 saturated fat, 60 mg sodium, 4 grams net carbs, 0 fiber, 2 grams sugar (0 added sugar), 4 grams protein

GF, Low Carb

Aquafaba Trade-Out /

The liquid drained from canned chickpeas can be used as a vegan egg-white replacer that whips to create a meringue-like foam.

Sully Sour

Inspired by The Chloe | NOLA

Makes 1 serving

Uptown mansion turned boutique hotel, The Chloe's story began in 1891 when renowned architect Thomas Sully was enlisted to design and build a home for a wealthy businessman. In the years to follow, the mansion would serve as a boardinghouse, then a bed and breakfast, before opening to the public as the majestic and welcoming Chloe.

INGREDIENTS

2 ounces Lapsang Souchong Peach Tea Concentrate, chilled (*recipe below*)

1 tablespoon lemon juice

1 tablespoon Raspberry Simple Syrup (*recipe on page 40*)

2 dashes fee foam (a vegan and zero proof foaming agent)

Pinch of ground pink Himalayan sea salt

Ice

3 raspberries, for garnish

Bamboo pick

METHOD

Combine all liquid ingredients and salt in a shaker tin and shake well. In a rocks glass, add ice. Pour contents of the shaker over ice and garnish with raspberries on bamboo pick.

LAPSANG SOUCHONG PEACH TEA CONCENTRATE

1 cup water

1 bag lapsang souchong tea

1 bag peach tea

METHOD

Bring water to a boil. Remove from heat and steep teas for 5-7 minutes. Do not squeeze the bags when removing.

NUTRITION

10 calories, 0 fat, 0 saturated fat, 120 mg sodium, 2 grams net carbs, 0 fiber, 0 sugar, 0 protein

GF, Vegan, Low Carb

Ingredient Swap /

Lapsang souchong is a black tea with a sweet yet smoky flavor and hints of pine resin, as pine is burned to smoke and dry the tea. If you don't have lapsang souchong available, just steep regular black tea along with the peach tea.

Patio Thyme

Inspired by Antoni's Italian Cafe | Acadiana

Makes 1 serving

Celebrated for their Italian cuisine, Antoni's makes the most of the fresh herbs grown right on their patio. This recipe infuses fresh thyme with tart grapefruit for a bubbly refresher.

INGREDIENTS

4 dashes Peychaud's bitters

3 tablespoons ruby red grapefruit juice

2 tablespoons Thyme Simple Syrup (*recipe below*)

Ice

4 ounces zero proof sparkling wine

Thyme sprig, for garnish

METHOD

Combine Peychaud's bitters, ruby red grapefruit juice, Thyme Simple Syrup, and ice in a shaker tin. Shake and double strain into a Collins glass. Add ice, then fill with zero proof sparkling wine. Garnish with fresh thyme.

THYME SIMPLE SYRUP

1 cup water

½ cup Swerve granular or 1½ cups granular allulose

½ cup loosely packed thyme sprigs

METHOD

In a small saucepan, bring water to a boil. Reduce to medium-high heat and add sweetener. Stir to dissolve and continue to heat for 10 minutes. Add thyme sprigs. Transfer to heat-safe glass container and allow to infuse for at least 1 hour. Double strain before using. Refrigerate unused portion in a sealed airtight container for up to 4 weeks.

NUTRITION

50 calories, 0 fat, 0 saturated fat, 0 sodium, 9 grams net carbs, 0 fiber, 7 grams sugar (0 added sugar), 0 protein

GF, Vegan, Low Carb

Raspberry Smash

Inspired by Cavan | NOLA

Makes 1 serving

It's like a sippable little SweeTart that's also incredibly refreshing.

INGREDIENTS

4 fresh raspberries (reserve 1 for garnish)

1 tablespoon Raspberry Simple Syrup (*recipe on page 40*)

2 tablespoons lemon juice

2 tablespoons orange juice

Crushed ice

3 basil leaves (reserve 1 for garnish)

Sparkling water, to top

Cocktail skewer

METHOD

In a rocks glass, muddle 3 raspberries with Raspberry Simple Syrup. Combine lemon juice and orange juice in a shaker tin with ice and shake vigorously. Add 2 basil leaves to tin and shake lightly to express the oils from the leaves without bruising. Strain into rocks glass and top with sparkling water. Gently stir and top with crushed ice. Garnish with remaining raspberry and basil leaf on cocktail skewer.

NUTRITION

30 calories, 0 fat, 0 saturated fat, 0 sodium, 6 grams net carbs, 1 gram fiber, 4 grams sugar (0 added sugar), 0 protein

GF, Vegan, Low Carb

Pro Tip /

Give basil leaves a quick slap to release aromatic oils.

Toddies + Teas

The medicinal powers of everyday ingredients such as tea, ginger, cinnamon, and anise not only nourish our bodies—they can also singlehandedly carry a cocktail. You have our permission, if you need it, to make these your own, mixing and matching personal favorite teas, herbs, and spices.

Cinnamon Anise Swizzle

Inspired by Citronola | NOLA

Makes 1 serving

This woody spice blend also qualifies as a medicinal libation, with cinnamon's blood-sugar-stabilizing effects and the digestive benefits of anise.

INGREDIENTS

4 ounces brewed Citronola Cinnamon Anise tea, chilled

2 tablespoons orange juice

Ice

Star anise ice cube (or 3 individual star anise)

Cinnamon stick, for garnish

Orange half-wheel, for garnish

METHOD

Combine Cinnamon Anise tea and orange juice in a small shaker tin with ice and shake vigorously. Double strain into novelty glass of choice. Add star anise ice cube, or use plain ice cubes and float 3 star anise on top. Garnish with cinnamon stick and orange half-wheel.

NUTRITION

20 calories, 0 fat, 0 saturated fat, 5 mg sodium, 5 grams net carbs, 0 fiber, 4 grams sugar (0 added sugar), 0 protein

GF, Vegan, Low Carb

Star Anise Ice Cubes /

Fill ice-cube trays halfway with Cinnamon Anise tea, add star anise to each, then freeze. Top off with water and freeze again.

Tip /

If Citronola isn't available near you, just use a blend of half cinnamon tea, half licorice tea instead.

Fever Dream

Inspired by Twelve Mile Limit | NOLA

Makes 1 serving

Harkening back to the days when alcohol was prescribed for medicinal purposes, this riff on a classic Hot Toddy actually just might help to clear congestion or soothe a sore throat. We also love it on a chilly evening, or even just when the A/C is blasting. Balanced, complex, and a little spicy, it's both piping hot and thirst quenching at the same time.

INGREDIENTS

1 tablespoon Swerve Brown Sugar

3 dashes Angostura bitters

1½ tablespoons lime juice

1½ ounces zero proof whiskey (we prefer Spiritless Kentucky 74)

4-5 ounces hot water

Lime swath, for garnish

METHOD

In a heat-safe mug, combine Swerve, Angostura bitters, lime juice, and zero proof whiskey. Stir with bar spoon, top with hot water, and garnish with lime swath.

NUTRITION

20 calories, 0 fat, 0 saturated fat, 5 mg sodium, 5 grams net carbs, 0 fiber, 1 gram sugar (1 gram added sugar), 0 protein

GF, Vegan, Low Carb

Ginger Tea-Ni

Inspired by Pyre Provisions | Northshore

Makes 1 serving

Centered on antioxidant-rich green tea and inflammation-quelching ginger, along with the alkalizing effects of fresh lemon juice, is there anything this drink *can't* do? If you want to do something good for your body, keep a pitcher of this on hand at all times.

INGREDIENTS

3 ounces brewed green tea, chilled

2 tablespoons Ginger Simple Syrup (*recipe on page 40*)

1 tablespoon lemon juice

Ice

Lemon swath, for garnish

METHOD

Combine green tea, Ginger Simple Syrup, and lemon juice in a small shaker tin filled with ice. Shake and double strain into a coupe glass. Squeeze lemon swath to express the oils, and twist to garnish.

NUTRITION

5 calories, 0 fat, 0 saturated fat, 0 sodium, 1 gram net carb, 0 fiber, 0 sugar, 0 protein

GF, Vegan, Low Carb

Pro Tip /

When peeling citrus, you'll want to slice only the most saturated color of the skin to release the sweet, aromatic oils. Including any part of the whiter rind will add an element of bitterness.

Elysian Fields

Inspired by Dickie Brennan's Steakhouse | NOLA

Makes 2 servings

> In Greek mythology, Elysian Fields is the beautifully peaceful place where the souls of the good went after death. Closer to home, Elysian Fields is a sprawling, tree-lined boulevard connecting Lake Pontchartrain to the Mississippi River, named after the Champs-Elysées in Paris, which translates to Elysian Fields.

INGREDIENTS

1 cup water

¼ cup granular allulose

½ cup blueberries

2 basil leaves

4 mint leaves (reserve 2 for garnish)

2 bags blueberry tea

2 tablespoons lime juice

6 ounces sparkling water

Ice

12 blueberries, for garnish

Bamboo picks

METHOD

In a medium saucepan, bring water to a boil and add allulose. Reduce to medium heat. Stir continuously until fully dissolved. Meanwhile, add blueberries to a small bowl and muddle. Remove saucepan from heat. Add muddled blueberries, basil, and mint and steep for 10 minutes. Add blueberry tea bags and steep for an additional 5 minutes.

Strain with a fine-mesh strainer into a heat-safe bowl. Refrigerate until cool. Add lime juice and stir.

Divide volume evenly between 2 glasses. Add sparkling water to taste, depending on desired level of sweetness. Gently stir and fill with ice. Garnish with mint leaves and fresh blueberries on bamboo picks.

NUTRITION

30 calories, 0 fat, 0 saturated fat, 15 mg sodium, 7 grams net carbs, 1 gram fiber, 5 grams sugar (0 added sugar), 0 protein

GF, Vegan, Low Carb

Tiki + Tropical

Grab your tiny paper umbrella and join us in whatever your version of paradise might be.

With any tiki drink, we believe in going unapologetically over the top. More is more is more. Go for bold colors and striking textures, and above all, garnish lavishly.

Watermelon Mint Martini

Inspired by Eliza Restaurant & Bar | Baton Rouge

Makes 1 serving

If you've ever wanted to cut open a watermelon and drink it on the spot, here's your chance. Containing more than 90 percent water and an excellent source of potassium, watermelon is a natural thirst quencher and quite possibly the perfect summertime "beverage."

INGREDIENTS

½ cup watermelon cubes

1½ ounces zero proof vodka

1½ tablespoons Citrea Oleo Saccharum (*recipe below*)

2 teaspoons lime juice

Ice

2 watermelon cubes, for garnish

2 lime wedges, for garnish

1 mint leaf, for garnish

Cocktail skewer

METHOD

In a blender, pulse watermelon until smooth. Combine watermelon, zero proof vodka, Citrea Oleo Saccharum and lime juice in a small shaker tin with ice. Shake and strain into a chilled glass. Garnish with skewer of alternating watermelon cubes, lime wedges, and mint leaf.

CITREA OLEO SACCHARUM

Makes approximately ¼ cup

1 cup lemon peels (approximately 6-8 lemons)

Zest of 2 lemons

⅓ cup granular allulose

Juice of 2 lemons

METHOD

In a medium mixing bowl, combine lemon peels, lemon zest, and allulose. Muddle every few minutes for approximately 15 minutes. Top with lemon juice and muddle periodically for another 15 minutes. Refrigerate as needed; double strain before using.

NUTRITION

35 calories, 0 fat, 0 saturated fat, 0 sodium, 10 grams net carbs, 0 fiber, 7 grams sugar (0 added sugar), 0 protein

GF, Vegan, Low Carb

Time Saver /

The process of making Citrea Oleo Saccharum is not for the faint of heart. If you're pressed for time, you can get by with simply adding 1 tablespoon Eat Fit Simple Syrup and the juice of half a lemon instead.

Piña Mambo

Inspired by Gris-Gris | NOLA

Makes 1 serving

> Floating (some may say *levitating*) the hibiscus tea in this gravity-defying libation is like doing a magic trick, every time

INGREDIENTS

⅛ orange with peel

4 mint leaves

2 tablespoons pineapple juice

Crushed or pellet ice

2 ounces brewed hibiscus tea, chilled

Mint sprig, for garnish

METHOD

Muddle orange and mint in a Collins glass. Add the pineapple juice, followed by crushed ice. Note that the crushed ice needs to be packed tightly into the glass, filling it completely. Slowly pour the hibiscus tea over the underside of a bar spoon, allowing for well-controlled precision in layering. Garnish with mint sprig.

NUTRITION

25 calories, 0 fat, 0 saturated fat, 0 sodium, 6 grams net carbs, 0 fiber, 5 grams sugar (0 added sugar), 0 protein

GF, Vegan, Low Carb

The Secret to Layering /

For starters, a tall skinny glass is ideal for showcasing the gorgeous separation in color. *Crushed* ice is essential for this technique to work, as it creates and maintains a natural barrier between the two liquids. Packing the crushed ice tightly is also key, filling the glass. Add the ingredients specifically in the order listed—denser ingredients first, followed by ice and then the slow hibiscus tea pour—to create and maintain the vivid separation in colors.

Kombucha Shipwreck

Inspired by Big Easy Bucha | NOLA

Makes 1 serving

The fresh pineapple isn't a deal breaker for this drink—we love the citrus effervescence just as much when served in a glass. Let's be honest, though; it's just way more festive to sip anything from a whole pineapple.

INGREDIENTS

1 pineapple

2 tablespoons orange juice

1 tablespoon lime juice

1 tablespoon Oleo Saccharum (*recipe on page 41*)

2 ounces zero proof rum

Ice

4 ounces Big Easy Bucha Florida Dreamin' (or any variation of citrusy kombucha)

Red cherry, for garnish

Orange half-wheel, for garnish

Edible flowers, for garnish

METHOD

Use a pineapple corer or paring knife to create a pineapple "shell" for serving vessel. Combine orange juice, lime juice, Oleo Saccharum, and zero proof rum in a shaker tin filled with ice. Shake well and strain into pineapple. Fill with kombucha, lightly stir, and garnish with cherry and orange half-wheel. Float edible flowers on top.

NUTRITION

80 calories, 0 fat, 0 saturated fat, 10 mg sodium, 19 grams net carbs, 1 gram fiber, 14 grams sugar (2 grams added sugar), 0 protein

GF, Vegan

Peach Frosé

Inspired by Gris-Gris | NOLA

Makes 4 servings

A frozen white sangria is never a bad thing, and it's even better when blended with a trio of fresh fruits.

INGREDIENTS

1 cup sliced strawberries

1 cup sliced peaches

4 pitted red cherries

1 bottle zero proof white zinfandel

3 tablespoons orange juice

2 tablespoons lime juice

1½ tablespoons granular allulose

Fresh fruit, for garnish

Bamboo picks

METHOD

In a blender, mix strawberries, peaches, and cherries until well combined, then pour into a large mixing bowl. Add three-quarters of the bottle of zero proof white zinfandel along with orange juice, lime juice, and allulose. Whisk lightly. Pour into a gallon zip-top bag and freeze for at least 6 hours or overnight.

When ready to blend, remove mixture from freezer and allow to thaw a bit at room temperature, about 15 to 20 minutes. Scoop the frozen mixture into blender and add splashes of the remaining wine, pulsing until it reaches a slushy consistency. Pour into glassware and garnish with fresh fruit on bamboo picks.

NUTRITION

90 calories, 0 fat, 0 saturated fat, 15 mg sodium, 22 grams net carbs, 2 grams fiber, 18 grams sugar (0 added sugar), 0 protein

GF, Vegan

Tip /

Fresh fruit is best, but frozen strawberries, peaches, and cherries can be used in a pinch.

Watermelon Juju

The Eat Fit Collection

Makes 1 serving

It's *just* like sipping a watermelon Jolly Rancher, in the best of ways—minus the sugar, and the Red 40 and Yellow 6, of course. Warning: first sip may induce childhood nostalgia.

INGREDIENTS

1 tablespoon Lyre's Zero Proof Orange Sec

2 tablespoons watermelon juice

3 dashes rhubarb bitters

1 tablespoon Eat Fit Simple Syrup (*recipe on page 39*)

1 tablespoon lemon juice

Crushed ice

Lemon wedge, for garnish

METHOD

Combine all liquid ingredients in a shaker tin filled with ice. Shake and double strain into a rocks glass over crushed ice. Garnish with lemon wheel.

NUTRITION

20 calories, 0 fat, 0 saturated fat, 0 sodium, 6 grams net carbs, 0 fiber, 5 grams sugar (2 grams added sugar), 0 protein

GF, Vegan, Low Carb

Watermelon Juice /

Buy it bottled, or make your own by blending ½ cup watermelon cubes until smooth, then strain with a fine-mesh sieve (or you can just use the puree, if you prefer your drink pulpy). Refrigerate unused portion for up to 72 hours.

Pucker Up Buttercup

The Eat Fit Collection

Makes 1 serving

It's delightfully crisp and totally tiki, with a bit of exotic spice and quite a pucker. You'll want to savor every last drop as you sip it up, Buttercup.

INGREDIENTS

2 tablespoons pear juice

1 ounce zero proof gin

1 tablespoon Eat Fit Simple Syrup (*recipe on page 39*)

1 tablespoon lemon juice

4 dashes Angostura bitters

Ice

4 mint leaves

4 ounces sparkling water

Lemon wheel, for garnish

Mint sprig, for garnish

METHOD

Combine all liquid ingredients, except for sparkling water, in a shaker tin with ice and mint leaves and shake. Double strain into a Collins glass. Top with sparkling water and ice. Gently stir and garnish with lemon wheel and mint sprig.

NUTRITION

25 calories, 0 fat, 0 saturated fat, 25 mg sodium, 5 grams net carbs, 0 fiber, 4 grams sugar (0 added sugar), 0 protein

GF, Vegan, Low Carb

Pear Juice /

Buy it bottled, or make your own by blending 1 pear (peeled and cubed) with ¼ cup water until smooth. Strain with a fine-mesh sieve. Refrigerate unused portion for up to 72 hours.

Index

F

G

H

K

L

M

N

O

P

Q

R

S

T

V

W

Z